10-88! OFFICER DOWN

The story of an officer involved shooting, politics, and his survival of Post-Traumatic Stress Disorder

by
Deputy Dustin A Reichert
Retired

10-88! OFFICER DOWN

The story of an officer involving shooting,
politics, and his survival of Post-Traumatic Stress Disorder

Printed in the United States of America

First Edition

ISBN   978-0692820568

Copyright © 2017 by Dustin A Reichert
www.DustinReichert.com
P.O. Box 490118
Blaine, MN 55449

Edited by Keidi Keating, www.YourBookAngel.com

For Tyealeen

I miss you, Sunshine

Thanks for the support!

#55

CONTENTS

DISCLAIMER

This book depicts actual events in the life of the author as truthfully as recollection permits and/or can be verified by research. This book is, first and foremost, a memoir. It reflects the author's present recollection and he has tried to recreate events, locals and conversations from author's memoirs, official investigation files and personal medical records. All persons within are actual individuals and there are no composite characters. Some events have been shortened and the names of some individuals have been changed. The reader should not consider this book anything other than a work of literature. This is a work of fiction, only in that in some cases, the author could not remember the exact words said by certain people, and exact descriptions of certain things, so gaps were filled in the best the author could. Otherwise, all characters and incidents and dialogue are real, are not products of the author's imagination, because at the time of this writing, the author had not imagination whatsoever for those kind of things.

The author would like to thank the real-life people portrayed in this book that brought comfort and support in some of the author's darkest times of his life. He recognizes that that the memoirs of others portrayed in this book might be different than his own. This book is not intended to hurt anyone. The author apologizes for any unintentional harm resulting from the publishing and marketing of *10-88! OFFICER DOWN*. This is a book of memory, and memory has its own story to tell. This book is a book of healing, and the healing has its own story to tell. The author has done his best to make it a truthful story.

ACKNOWLEDGEMENTS

Thank you to Jacob, my oldest son. It was your face that ran through my mind in the moments after I got shot and led to all my decisions on survival. I couldn't bear the idea of you having to grow up without me.

Thank you to Deputy Samantha Cruze. You were my friend before the shooting, and after this painful journey, we found our way back to that friendship. You risked your life to stay with me even though you thought I was dead. I cherish that and your bravery. But I cherish our friendship much more.

Thank you to my wife, my kids, my mother, and the rest of family and close friends as they had to ride this thirteen-year rollercoaster ride. The true friendships were the ones whose light shined through all the darkness.

Thank you to my brothers and sisters of the badge who came to my rescue that morning and handled the various angles of rescue and investigation, as well as those who helped me at various stages through my healing.

Thank you to the dispatchers for your professional calm during this intense event.

Thank you to Attorney Marylee Abrams. It may have been your job, but your taking my case personal reassured me that you were handling each step with full effort.

Last, and certainly not least, thank you to Sheriff James Stuart for finally allowing me to heal. You are forever a friend. May God bless you and your family as much as you have blessed me.

FOREWORD

Dustin is one of the few people who intimately know the ultimate fight concerning when someone is trying to kill you. Hardworking police officers such as Dustin live in an alternate universe – the one nobody wants to visit, let alone experience. While most people's knowledge of the police universe is represented from brief overlaps of traffic citations or victimizations (neither particularly pleasant encounters), even fewer are aware of the dangerous and serious world of man's inhumanity to man, which is a regular duty tour for police officers.

Dustin's deadly encounter began as most police calls typically do – responding to someone's call for help, which often involves going toward the danger. While it was 'just' a loud music complaint, this particular call turned bad quickly. While approaching the brown duplex, the crazed homeowner with a gun appeared, pointing that gun right at Dustin. Things turned bad fast. Shots were exchanged and an officer was down in an instant. The threat neutralized at the same time.

The initial fight was now over, Dustin being critically injured with two close-range gunshot wounds, the attacker dead, and Dustin's partner uninjured. A series of lifesaving efforts ensued by other police department members, EMS personnel, doctors, and extensive hospital staff ultimately saved Dustin's life and returned him to a functional state whereby he eventually returned to duty. One might think this completes the entire story of this nightmare adventure – but they would be wrong in this assumption.

While Dustin did his best to heal and return to duty, the medical damage of his bullet injuries took a permanent toll, and ultimately caused him to retire. Statistically, officers involved in a shooting leave police work in significantly greater numbers whether they were injured or simply participated as a shooter. There are several key reasons for these departures from a 'blue career,' ranging from physical and mental injuries, a personal family reevaluation, or other internal and external factors. The department's handling of Dustin in terms of investigation and administrative policies (and lack thereof in some cases) turned less than ideal and became an extended ordeal of its own. A steady stream of evaluations – medical, orthopedic, psychological, and department 'fitness-for-duty' aspects were a continuing effort with which Dustin had to contend. Add to this the plethora of insurance and retirement hurdles, not to mention the various financial costs that it took to hold Dustin and his family's life together. All of this became 'part two' of an initial shooting event that took seconds, which has taken years in an effort to become whole and begin a new life beyond Dustin's heroism and chosen police career.

ne of the quiet police 'truisms' is that all cops know each other, even if we have not met face-to-face. Within that construct, we all know the job of police work, what happens 'out there,' and what we all go through. I first met Dustin electronically, years after his shooting, his medical retirement, and his administrative ordeal, yet it was like I have known him all along. Dustin was on a higher education quest and found himself in one of my college classes at a major university through the technology of online distance education. In our time together, we both communicated to each other like life-long friends (it's a 'cop' thing) and we quickly understood each other's careers, and 'had each other's backs' as Dustin dove in to upscale scholarship – one of his new life goals.

I have learned many things in my time with Dustin. He is an awesomely pleasant, honest, and driven man. While Dustin has plenty of negatives to dwell on, he fastidiously chooses to keep moving forward, and he has forged a career in motivational speaking to bestow his hard-earned knowledge of life's gifts to others. In one of his main messages, Dustin embodies that bad things happen to good people – either intentionally or unintentionally – but, the best possible outcome in both cases is to move forward, to grow, to excel, and to continue to enjoy life's gifts. It has been my sincere pleasure to personally get to know Dustin and revel at his amazing journey – and there is no stopping him. I suspect you will find the same.

By Sgt. Gary Apperson
Anchorage Police Dept. (ret)
Criminal Justice Adjunct Professor, MSCJ.

PROLOGUE

The idea of writing this book kept coming to my mind ever since May, 2003. I initially had the idea to write my story about a year after it had happened, but I didn't know why or how to go about it. Every person I've encountered since that day has wanted to know specific details about the shooting. They have wanted to know how I dealt with nearly dying, how I dealt with taking someone's life, and how my agency responded and treated me after. But anytime I shared that I suffered from Post-Traumatic Stress Disorder (PTSD), the desire to learn more often seemed to end. I don't think it was out of rudeness, but more because of the misunderstanding of PTSD and its stigma. If I shared how the main cause of my PTSD was the handling of the shooting by my Agency, and how they treated me, unless I was talking to another Police Officer, the conversation would usually cease.

When most people think of a police shooting, they usually believe that the biggest battle is when the bullets are flying. In reality, that is only the start of the real battle that most officers go through, and this was certainly true in my case. I am sharing my story so people can understand more about my own experience, during a time when public misconception about the dynamics of police use of force and shootings is at an all-time high. I hope people can learn from this experience and gain a better understanding of the deeper aspects of traumatic incidences and dealing with PTSD. My true hope is that administrations from Police and Sheriff's Departments from across the country can better grasp the impact of their actions, and inactions, when it comes to traumatic events such as police shootings.

Most importantly, I am putting my story to paper as a part of my continued path to healing.

PART 1
Pathway to the Badge

CHAPTER 1
"THIS IS HOW IT STARTS"

It was a peaceful moonlit night on the night of May 12, 2003 until the radio exploded:

"4A57 Shots Fired…Officer Down…Officer Down…Shots Fired…10-88." That was coming from the radio of Deputy Samantha (Sam) Cruze, my friend and partner that night.

4A57 was the number assigned to the Andover Power Shift Car, and 3A40 was the call sign assigned to the Andover C Shift Car. The first number of the call sign indicated the shift, 3 being "C shift," or overnights. The 4 meant it was a "power car," meaning it was an overlapping shift, in this case a 7:00 p.m. to 3:30 a.m. shift. The letter indicates the area you are assigned, in this case the "A" was assigned as Andover. The last two numbers were to identify that particular unit or Deputy. 10-88 is the universal Minnesota radio code for an officer in an emergency situation. That radio transmission was followed by a series of tones designed to indicate an emergency situation.

After the tones are heard, Dispatch broadcasts, "Information for cars, Office Down in Andover. 2118 140th Lane…Officer Down…Ambulance En Route." Shortly after you hear

3

Dispatch asking if there was any further information or suspect description. Deputy Cruze responded:

"Male in his twenties with a gun. He's inside the townhouse, 1 house east of the [callers] address. I think 3A40's down, I'm not sure. Male possibly armed with a handgun."

This, of course, was followed by a series of officers calling out on their radios that they were en route. There is nothing more heart wrenching for a police officer than when one of their own is in trouble. Officers from the Anoka County Sheriff's Office, Anoka Police Department, Coon Rapids Police Department, Blaine Police Department, Ramsey Police Department, St. Francis PD and Columbia Heights all responded to the call. Word got out quickly and officers from State Patrol, Ramsey County, and Hennepin County were also en route to assist in any way they could. Sam later told me that even Minneapolis and St. Paul officers were on the scene and it was more amazing than I could ever imagine. She said it seemed like all those squads arrived in seconds. When I later learned of the overwhelming response from all the different agencies, I couldn't believe it. I was humbled.

It's interesting to share this story because, in order to do so, I had to refresh myself by listening to the dispatch recordings of that night and reading the news clips. I usually don't shed a tear over the shooting all year long anymore, only sometimes on the anniversary, but hearing the recording of my partner and friend, Deputy Samantha Cruze, calling out and stressed on the radio, and hearing the response from the Dispatchers and Officers coming to rescue me, gets me every time. Most people think the stress and trauma inside me come from the shooting itself, yet there are many more feelings and emotions involved with an officer getting shot than anyone can understand. Therefore, as most people fortunately haven't had to deal with being shot, not many people understand. It's finally time to open my heart and mind and share the whole story.

So, I am wiping away those tears and graciously and humbly sharing my story with you.

CHAPTER 2
I ALWAYS WANTED TO BE A COP

Okay, maybe not *always*, but certainly from an early age in life. My parents divorced before I was one year old, so a split family life was normal for me. My first memory of a police officer was when we lived in Ramsey, Minnesota, in a rural area. I was about five years old and my mom was dating a guy named "Bear." Bear liked his pills and alcohol. I don't know the reason why, but I remember Bear went crazy one night and beat my mom up pretty bad. He threw a bottle at her so hard that, although it missed her head, it lodged into the wall. Eventually the police and the ambulance turned up and swept my mom away. I don't remember seeing Bear after that. But I do remember how comforting the police were to me and my older brother. I don't know for sure if that incident prompted me to want to be a police officer. Hell, I'm fairly confident that almost every little boy thinks about being either a police officer or a firefighter.

When I was six years old, my mom, my brother, and I moved to the North Side of Minneapolis, Minnesota. When my mom first found the house in Minneapolis, they told her it was an "Urban Redevelopment Area," which really meant they would find dilapidated houses, tear them down, and rebuild new houses. We didn't live in a recently built house, but rather a "fixer-upper" built in 1890 that took a few years to fix up. It was a very poor neighborhood and increasingly violent with a surge of Chicago gang members coming to Minneapolis. I lived across the street from Farview Park, so at least we had a place to go and be safe, except for the periodic moments where I would get punched, beat up a little, or even robbed. As upsetting as these things were, I accepted it all as a part of life. Because for anyone growing up in these neighborhoods, that was life. Except for the elderly white folks who had lived there for decades, it was pretty much a neighborhood with a high ratio of Black residents, Native Americans, some Laotians, and a few of us "White Boys." I assimilated well so I had friends of all colors and nationalities. My mom later joked that I always brought a rainbow of friends to the house, happy that I had a racially diverse group of friends. As I got older, a large amount of my friends were black and, although I didn't join any gangs, I was protected from most of the gang bangers who would try to prey on me as one of the few white kids in the neighborhood. In the late seventies and eighties, the Minneapolis Public Schools decided to integrate the schools more, so many students from "the minority area" were bused to the "white schools." I was bused to Northeast Minneapolis throughout Elementary and Middle School. Because of that I got separated from some of my closest friends and had to attend a school across the river. I didn't like it there, but those experiences prepared me for my later life and career in Law Enforcement.

My mom eventually met and married my stepfather, Phil, who was a U.S. Customs Agent at the time. I was around eight years old when they met. I fondly remember the first time he drove me around the neighborhood in his unmarked squad car with a red light magnetically attached to the top. It was pretty exciting. My birth father Fred, lived in Waukesha, Wisconsin, a suburb of Milwaukee, and I spent a part of my summers there almost every year. He had a police scanner at his apartment, which he left on 24-7. There always seemed to be something going on in that little town of Waukesha. I loved listening to the police scanner. I would sit in the chair by it for hours listening to the "action" of little old Waukesha. Sometimes I would fall asleep on the couch as I listened. I think that is what ignited my desire to become a police officer. If something was going on close enough for the squads to come by blaring their red lights and sirens, I was in heaven as my imagination went wild about the unknown details. Unfortunately, I never got to find out how the incidents would end. And that is what I always desired.

Fast forward to the late 1980's when we lived in Minnetonka, Minnesota, where we moved part of the way through my Freshman year of high school. My mom and stepdad worked hard to be able to afford to move us to a nicer area. I went from living in a very poor, mostly black neighborhood, to a mostly white neighborhood, where I struggled to fit in with the almost all white student body, in a high school of over 1400 students, and more than 400 in my class alone. North High School, the one I just transferred from, had a total of 500 students in the entire school. It was a bit of a culture shock and overwhelming for me. During the first year, I refused to be anything or anyone different than how I knew myself to be. But that held me back socially and I realized that we all change as we grow because of those around us. I eventually made many friends from a variety of social groups and broke a lot of social barriers. And it was nice to worry less about violence and stealing like I had to in Minneapolis.

Junior year came along and I learned to drive. I had a love-hate relationship with the local Law Enforcement. I was still interested with it all, but as a teen driver I found the police to be my enemy. It seemed to me that they were always picking on teens and involved in "speed traps." When I got older, I realized I just needed to slow down and drive the speed limit. A wonderful new TV show started airing in early 1989. It was the "original reality TV" show and aired on Fox Network. They simply called it "Cops." This unscripted TV show can still be seen today as reruns, although it was cancelled in 2013. I was hooked from the very first episode I watched. I loved to look into people's lives, the officers, and the citizens they interacted with. I loved the way my heart raced and adrenalin pumped as officers rushed to calls, getting in fights, and chasing on foot and in car. I loved seeing the real personalities of police officers, which are different than we all perceived them to be when interacting with them. Since the show was aired on Saturday nights, I delayed going out that night with my friends or girlfriend until after Cops had finished. More than once my girlfriend at the time would sit on the couch waiting for me, forced to watch Cops before we went out. My stepdad, who was now retired as a US Customs Agent, would sit in his chair watching it too. I was totally addicted, as was he, and shortly after that I felt like I wanted to be a police officer.

I often spoke about wanting to be a police officer to my mom, my stepdad, and also to my dad. My mom always brought up how good I am at sales and business. She *did not* want me to be a police officer and would try to divert my attention. My dad wasn't fond of the idea either, but because of issues with alcoholism and absence in our early lives, he would go with any reasonable thoughts I had to try and make up for lost times. My stepdad was pretty supportive of the idea of me entering Law Enforcement, although he wasn't a fan of my original hopes to be a Drug Enforcement Administration (DEA) Agent. But he thought I was a lazy teen so I'm sure he figured I would never take it that far.

After high school my mom was transferred for work and we moved to Kingwood, Texas, a suburb of Houston. I trailed along because I wasn't ready to afford life on my own yet. My mom had talked me into pursuing a business degree in college. She pushed the fact that I was good at sales and would be a great business leader. Then one day I was sitting in class listening to my business teacher talk about "widgets" (his word to describe a production in any theory we are discussing). And then it hit me*... this shit isn't for me....I want to be a cop.* I had already been asking local Harris County Constables who patrolled my city about the job and was deeply considering it. I discussed changing degrees with my counselor and then we made it happen. I was now a Criminal Justice student! I went home and told my mom that day and she wasn't thrilled. But my mom is a kind and loveable woman... and very understanding. She's also very blunt and she was pretty direct with me. I remember seeing tears well up in her eyes. At some point, early in my new career she said to me, "Promise me you'll always come home, every night." Of course, I responded, "I promise

Mom," and we hugged. My brother had died in a car accident years before and she didn't want to lose her only living child. Later in my career I used that as part of my motivation to always go home after each shift.

In 1994, I moved back to Minnesota, my true home. I graduated from Inver Hills Community College with an Associate Degree in Law Enforcement with a Minor in Criminal Justice. I had finally gotten into the Peace Officers Standards and Training Board Skills (POST) program and for the first time in my life, I was an A and high B student. This was absolutely for me. I enjoyed the subject matter, I thrived off of the competition, and I was training for my dream job. As a matter of fact, a few classmates and I started a competition, suggested by fellow Cadet Michael Treat, to battle for Top Gun based on shooting, accuracy, and other factors. I was certainly not the most accurate with the gun, but somehow, I pulled off the Top Gun Award. The original discussion was that whoever won would have their dinner and bar tab paid for by the rest of the class, but very few of the class agreed to that part, as I guess they were all broke. As fun as that was, it wasn't the award I was going after; it was the enjoyment of learning and being natural at something.

While attending college, I did an internship with the Ramsey County Sheriff's Office. I was exposed to multiple divisions and saw many aspects to Law Enforcement, much more than most agencies were offering in internships for college students. I started in the jail, rode with Civil Division serving papers, the Warrants and Transports Division, the Jail Unit at Regions Hospital and, finally, in the Patrol Division. There

I got my first exposure to police shootings and the various after effects. Of the various Deputies that I rode with, one of them was K9 Handler Deputy Ed Whitledge and his dog, Duke. I had met him previously when I was riding with other Deputies, but now it was my time to ride with a K9 officer. Deputy Whitledge was very informative and knowledgeable during the shift.

He wasn't a huge man or tall, only about 5'10". He was quiet, but his personality was large. He had a certain intensity to him. I could tell a part of his mind was always spinning and processing thoughts. As quiet and guarded as he was, Deputy Whitledge seemed to open up to me fairly quickly. Maybe it was because I was an outside person or because he wanted to protect me as I worked towards earning a badge myself. Maybe he was subtly trying to tell me that I might want to reconsider my career choice. Who knows?

During our conversations while patrolling, he suddenly stopped talking. We were passing an apartment building in the city of Little Canada at the time, but weren't on a call or anything. Suddenly he stopped, gave me a strange look, and said, "You want to see something?"

I said, "Yes, of course," figuring he was going to show me some juicy Law Enforcement stuff. That's exactly what he shared, but much more than I expected. As we pulled past the garages for this particular apartment building, he showed me a garage door with a couple of panels on them that had obviously been replaced. They were of mismatching colors. He said, "Those are from a shooting I was in." Deputy Whitledge explained how he and another Deputy were responding to a call of shots fired in the area. As he and his partner searched the area, along with his K9 partner Bud, the other Deputy saw someone he thought had a "long gun," (a rifle or shotgun). They searched that area more and found an unlocked garage door. They opened it to investigate further. Inside there was room for two vehicles nose to nose but there was only a single car. After yelling commands for anyone in there to come out, Deputy Whitledge sent K9 Bud in to check the stall further.

With a crack in his voice, he said a flash of light and single shot from what turned out to be a sawed-off shotgun came from the darkness. The shotgun pellets hit K9 Bud, killing him instantly, and splattering blood all over Whitledge's face and uniform. He described the gory details further, but they aren't important for this book. Deputy Whitledge said both Deputies returned fire, with Deputy Whitledge emptying his gun, and the suspect ultimately dying. He didn't share a ton about the experience afterward except for making it clear that the post shooting handling was pretty stressful from the administrative response as well as the criminal and civil review. And he said the fact that the county had to pay for a new door but the complex owner had fixed it in the cheapest way possible by only replacing a couple of panels, meant he was forced to see that visual reminder often. "Sometimes it's the little things that bother you the most," he said. Almost ten years later I truly understood what he meant because of my own shooting.

I could see that talking about that incident upset him and he became quiet. After a long pause he said he was in the Vietnam War. He followed with, "When I was in Vietnam, I expected this, but when you come home you don't expect to be in war on the streets." That was a pretty powerful statement. I thanked him for sharing his story and we went on to Patrol other areas. Although he never spoke about it again that night, his story resonated in my mind. It was the single most valuable thing I would learn on my internship. I later learned from some of his close friends that he was constantly questioned by administration and even his partners about the emptying of his hand gun and his actions that night. There were no criminal charges filed and he was cleared of any wrongdoing. But knowing what I know now about traumatic incidences and the studies about the need for support, I can only imagine the toll it took on him.

After becoming part-time licensed with Ramsey County on the Lakes and Trails Unit, I interacted with Deputy Whitledge often. He was always outgoing to me, but I noticed his intensity increased each time I saw him. His eyes would often bulge out and be keen to everything going on around him. He retired in 1999. Deputy Whitledge died of a heart attack ten years later at the age of 58. He was a prime example of how much Traumatic Stress, including handling after the fact, can take a toll on a Police Officer's career and health.

The Ramsey County Sheriff's Department had a Reserve Unit, The Lakes and Trails Unit, which I mentioned earlier. I had considered this option in Houston, so I was excited to finally make it happen. Ramsey County allows you to work towards becoming a part-time licensed Deputy and not only be able to work volunteer events, but also some paid boat and snowmobile patrols. In my three and a half years there I worked in roles from a Reserve Deputy to a part-time licensed Deputy to a full-time licensed Deputy working part-time, sometimes for pay, sometimes volunteering. I worked Water Patrol, Snowmobile Patrol, Park Patrol, ATV Patrol, Community Events, and I was an instructor for Water Safety, Snowmobile Safety and ATV Safety. I often worked the details that involved actual Law Enforcement duties, such as Park Patrols in St. Paul to further my learning. I eventually reached the rank of Sergeant on my unit, but it's not as impressive as it sounds. In reality, it meant I got first picks of details I signed up for, and I was in charge of the squad car I drove during my shifts. I also had to keep track of my group of volunteers to make sure they were putting in their volunteer time, and help get the sign ups filled.

My experiences with Ramsey County taught me a lot, but my goal was to become a regular law enforcement officer. During my time with the Lakes and Trails Unit I got a lot of experience but only one real incident tested my resolve in the criminal justice world. I was working in Battle Creek Park, which has parts both in St. Paul and in Maplewood, all within my county. It was late and my partner and I were doing one final pass through before we headed back to the Patrol Station to call it a night. It was after the park was closed and we came upon a car parked on the side of the road with a single occupant in it. My partner was an unlicensed reserve so I took the lead on the stop. After calling it out over my radio to dispatch, I asked the man to exit the vehicle. As we were chatting he was acting really nervous and he wouldn't look at me. I was still pretty inexperienced but he was sending out all kinds of red flags. He was a white male and fairly tall and stocky. He had on dirty clothing, long dirty hair, and refused to look me in the eye. Although I'm tall at almost 6'3", I was a pretty scrawny guy at that age. I had dispatch do a check for wants and warrants and sure enough he had a warrant out of Anoka County. That part was pretty ironic since I had been at Anoka County Jail less than a week later getting fingerprinted for a background check as part of my application process. We were standing behind his car and in front of my squad at this point. When I told the suspect he was under arrest, he immediately pulled away from me and ran to his car, opening the driver's door. I caught up with him right away. He seemed to want to get in that car pretty bad and I wanted him to stay out pretty bad so we got into a physical struggle. As he kept reaching in, he seemed to be focusing on the underside of the front seat. Finally, I pulled him out enough that I was able to slam the door on his hand. That was enough to get him to stop fighting and he took off running on foot.

Running is not my thing. I would go so far as to say that I HATE RUNNING AND I ALWAYS HAVE! He took off and went up a busy road. I did my best to keep up with him but my energy was draining fast. My partner whizzed past me because he was in much better shape. The problem though, was that my partner wasn't armed. Finally, a car pulled up and inside it was a woman with her child. She asked, "Can I help with anything? Can I give you a ride?" I gladly accepted and told her to drive. I could barely speak I was so out of breath and by this time it looked like my partner had run out of energy too. But he kept going, now just jogging to try to keep up with the suspect. We drove past the suspect and then I jumped out of the car, which caused him to turn and run into the wooded area. I was calling things out to my dispatch at this point but I was in the St. Paul Police area and too far away from my Sheriff's partners. All I could do was hope it was being shared with St. Paul PD in a timely fashion. As we ran through the woods he tripped in a concrete drain path for rainwater. I jumped on him and he wouldn't stop fighting. The Dispatcher on that night was a very experienced woman named Julie, who adored me. She told me later she felt so worried. She kept asking for updates in the middle of the fight. And my rookie ass kept answering! Finally, I yelled out over the radio, "Standby, I'm fighting here!" He started fighting even harder, punching at me and grabbing near my belt. I knew I was almost out of energy too and considered shooting him at that point. I had a hold of his hair and finally I smacked his head on the concrete drain path a few times during the fight to get him to stop. On the third smack he finally stopped fighting, right about the time St. Paul Police showed up to assist me. They got him out of the wooded area for me so I could process it all and breathe again. Knowing what I know now about drugs, and because of the nature of his warrants, he was most likely high on Methamphetamine, which gave him an edge on me. When we searched the car, under the front seat I found a very large hunting knife. My normal Sergeant wasn't on at the time so I asked the Patrol Sergeant to review my report since I had never used force before and I was nervous. I knew it was all okay when he looked up at me and replied, "I'd have cracked his skull open with my flashlight. Good job."

During the time I was entering the field of Law Enforcement, it was saturated with candidates. Simply getting into the Law Enforcement Skills Program took three times of applying since it was on a lottery system and I wasn't an A-student yet. Once I took the Peace Officers Standards and Training (POST) Board test, which was the licensing board for Police Officers in Minnesota, I was able to apply to a variety of agencies throughout the state, but I would often be one of three hundred people applying for one or two open positions. My original goal was to either be a Saint Paul Police Officer or a Minnesota State Trooper. As time passed, I started to not care about where I got a job, as long as I finally got a full-time police officer job, which finally came in August 1998 when I was hired as a full-time Deputy for the Anoka County Sheriff's Office.

CHAPTER 3
I'M FINALLY A COP!

I was sworn in with the Anoka County Sheriff's Office on August 28, 1998 and I couldn't have been happier. I had anticipated being hired with the Ramsey County Sheriff's Department since I had done my internship and Reserve service with them. I even got a letter from Ramsey County Sheriff Bob Fletcher, whom I had interacted a lot with during my time there, encouraging me to apply and test for the next open position with the Ramsey County Sheriff's Department. But truthfully, I liked the idea of not having to work in the Jail for several years before going to Patrol, which was pretty much a given with Ramsey County. I'm more of a high-energy action-oriented kind of guy, so the jail isn't my thing, unless, of course, I'm bringing someone there to be booked. And this was a job that I had finally been offered so I wasn't going to turn that down. I had worked too hard at that point.

My Swearing-In Ceremony was probably one of the proudest days of my life. My mom lived in the Washington DC area at the time and she had a work commitment and couldn't make it to the Swearing-In, but both my dad and stepdad made it. They were both so supportive during my Law Enforcement Schooling and in life in general. Also present was my one-and-a-half-year-old son, his mom, and a couple of friends. When Sheriff Larry Podany, who was my Sheriff when I got hired, asked who I was going to have pin my badge on, I asked both my dad and stepdad to step up, which was led mostly by my dad. When I look at the pictures from that day, I can see the pride in both of their eyes, as well as in my own.

I was assigned to the Patrol Division. Field Training involved four phases where you are assigned to three different Field Training Officers (FTOs), and the FTO for Phases one and four was generally the same. Deputy Tony Fitzloff was my Phase one and four FTO. Tony was a hoot! He had been with the department for quite some time. He was a short guy with a receding light brown hair line and a mustache. He reminded me of Detective Sipowicz from NYPD Blue, only a lot jollier mostly. He was a stickler about geography and I sucked at geography. I struggled because I grew up in areas that had street numbers in sequence, not names. And in Anoka County the streets were named after trees, flowers, birds, and presidents. He sure hounded me, but we shared lots of laughs, and I think he was the perfect base to start my training. He definitely strengthened my geographical knowledge of the county.

Phase 2 was with Deputy Tom Struzinski. The training style and attitudes were night and day in comparison to Deputy Fitzloff. Deputy Struzinski was an intense individual. He was on the tall side, but not as tall as me and he had a very thin frame. Deputy Struzinski had an intense look in his eyes and he didn't hesitate to raise his voice. There weren't a lot of laughs during that four weeks. He smoked a lot, and as much as I hated the smell of cigarette smoke I gladly asked him many times during a shift if he wanted a smoke break.

At least a cigarette would calm him down and make the shift less stressful for both of us. I went home most nights when working with him and it would take me at least two hours to wind down from the tension and stress the eight-and-a-half-hour shift with Deputy Struzinski would cause. That said, he was a very good FTO and had lots of knowledge to share. He was the first Deputy that piqued my interested in focusing on the local drug problem. I believe his style prepared my ego for dealing with the attitudes of the people on the streets.

Phase three was probably my most miserable phase. It was C Shift, which is 10:00 p.m. to 6:30 a.m. with Deputy Bob Elmer. Deputy Elmer wasn't the most aggressive Deputy on the department and I was at a phase where I felt I would have a bit of freedom on traffic and the likes. But that messed with his patrol style, so I sucked it up. It was his squad. He had a great personality and we shared a lot of laughs together. As my career progressed, I realized the importance of the ability to laugh away some of the stresses of the job.

Phase four is an evaluation phase, and I was back with my original FTO and mentor, Deputy Fitzloff. I was proud to be let off Phase four a couple of days early, graduating my training. This was more common at that time since we were shorter on staffing. It was more of a slap in the face at the time if you couldn't reach an early release during that last week of FTO. It was official, I was a full-fledged, full-time Deputy... on probation, but it still felt great!

My initial assignment was working in both the City of Oak Grove and Countywide. I worked half my week assigned to Oak Grove and the rest of the week Countywide, switching between the east side and west side. Deputy Fitzloff and Struzinski, my training officers, were proactive in enforcement and both taught me quite a bit about the local shit bag areas, and there were many of them in the City of Oak Grove back then. There is a road called Sims Road that runs through Oak Grove and East Bethel. But to local Methers it was known as Meth Highway or Crank Avenue because at most times of the day you could find someone to buy Methamphetamine (Meth, Crank, Dope, Crystal) from within two blocks in either direction, as long as you knew the right people.

Prior to working with Anoka County, I had an internship and continued to work with and volunteer with a group called Hand In Hand. Their focus was on Street Gangs, conducting research on the street and providing presentations and trainings, and they even presented a detailed report to the Minnesota Legislature on the current state of Street Gangs in Minnesota. Most of my work involved collecting and analyzing data on graffiti and tagger crews, including collecting photos. I would also help during confidential interviews, called "oral histories," of members of these crews, and the members of known and violent street gangs. This was originally an internship position for my four-year degree, but I continued to work with Hand In Hand after that internship expired. Ultimately they published a report for the Minnesota Legislature that I was proud to be a part of. The expertise of the Research Directors, Kate Cavett and St.

Paul Lieutenant, eventually Police Chief John Harrington, were invaluable to my learning and understanding of gangs. And more importantly, to building my base needed to focus and specialize in certain criminal justice angles. Because of this affiliation and my desire to find myself in the action, I had hoped that gangs would be my focus in Law Enforcement. However, although there were gang members in Anoka County, there wasn't a strong gang problem, especially in the Northern Anoka County where I was assigned, so that didn't transpire to be my focus. I continued to work the Oak Grove, East Bethel, and St. Francis area for most of my first three years with Anoka County and one thing which became apparent was that there was a serious drug issue in the area, specifically with methamphetamine, marijuana, and alcohol. I needed a new focus and I had found one.

I'm someone who likes to dive into learning core specialties when working a job and this was solidified during my time with Hand In Hand. I began to focus my training, learning, and enforcement focus in an area that Anoka County obviously had a problem in, which was drugs and alcohol. I watched videos, read official websites, read books, monitored drug user websites, and asked to attend any drug or alcohol related training. Most of my partners at the time weren't interested in most of the trainings I attended, but I found a couple of ways to make it happen. You had to put any training request into your Sergeant. Whether the request would be forwarded or not depended on the Sergeant assigned to you. So I would do a memo about the training to my Sergeant, but also CC the training Lieutenant and training secretary. I would also offer to go on my days off to certain trainings if they paid for the training, which they often agreed to, but they still gave me comp time. Then I finally convinced them to let me be the first Deputy for Anoka County to become a Certified Drug Recognition Expert (DRE). It was the most intensive training I had ever experienced overseen by the International Association of Chiefs of Police. It was a fantastic training. The DRE's most common role is to do evaluations on subjects suspected of driving under the influence of drugs. We spent three intensive weeks doing classroom work and the next two weeks finding subjects under the influence, doing the evaluation and then a urine confirmation. I was proud to officially be a Drug Recognition Expert.

My street drug arrests and meth lab arrests were pretty high and I finally earned a spot on the Anoka Hennepin Violent Crimes and Drug Task Force. It was only a temporary stint since someone was on tour in Iraq, but it was an honor to be chosen and an opportunity to prove myself for when a full opening came up. "Do good and you'll come back when the regular spot opens up next year" is what my new Lieutenant told me. I was kind of a "nerd" on the task force but with the regular position on the line, I had to be. I dug into the equipment available and became as knowledgeable as possible with the various equipment we had. I even volunteered to keep a laptop and portable printer in my undercover squad so we could type and print search warrants on location wherever we were. I received a lot of flack from the others when typing on scene because they said I took too long, but I would often tell them, with love, "Hey jackass, I've never had a judge question or turn down one of my warrants, or overturned in court. Back off!" There was little argument with them after that. We were rough on each other, but it was all done with fun. I also kept on top of my daily caseload paperwork, which wasn't easy. I wanted to be looked at as an asset to make things easier when deciding if I would come back in the fall. It can get a bit chaotic with a bunch of police officers from multiple agencies who grow their hair out, work undercover, deal with druggies all day long, work crap hours, and have lots of down time. It wasn't easy to get paperwork done at the office, especially being the newest Detective. Practical jokes, blowing off steam, and the loveable Drug K9 Cleo made getting work done in the office nearly impossible. Often I would come into the office on Sundays when no one was there and grind out most of my paperwork.

I really enjoyed my time on the Task Force, which felt like a natural fit for me. My knowledge of drugs and the drug world was pretty solid so the learning curve was fairly easy. Detective Dan Pelkey, Blaine Police Officer, was assigned to get me up to speed on things at the Task Force. We were friends anyway and graduated in the same Law Enforcement Skills Program in college, which made the transition process a little smoother for me. We stayed pretty tight partners on many cases during my time there. My first case was a garbage search where a different detective followed up on information and searched the garbage to the address, finding enough evidence for a search warrant. It was "just a marijuana case" so it was a smaller risk and was not supposed be much, so she was glad to turn it over to me. Well that little case turned into a federal case when a person walked in on the search warrant with four and a half ounces of pure powdered cocaine. I will never forget watching the large package of pure white substance slide across the floor as he was being taken down. My first official case as Lead Detective ended up with multiple other arrests and prison time for the suspect who walked in on the warrant.

My first undercover work buying drugs wasn't so successful though. It was a case Detective Skip Standel was originally working and had me be the Undercover Officer (UC). Detective Standel had received information about a male trading blow jobs from other males for discounted "8 balls" of methamphetamine. An 8 ball is the street slang term for 3.5 grams of substance. I knew I was getting this detail because I was the new guy on the task force. Either because the others didn't want to do it or I was getting hazed. Or maybe a combination of both. I was just hoping they didn't give some extra delay when I did the bust word just to mess with me. One of my patrol partners from ACSO was also a Detective on the Task Force. I was told she did a lot of undercover work so I asked her what to say or ask for when I got to the door if he answered. She told me to ask him if he "had any white." I hadn't heard that term and I should have known better because I had a lot more drug education and experience overall. But I think the overwhelmed thoughts about doing my first undercover allowed the concern to slip past me.

I got out from the surveillance vehicle around the corner from the target house I started walking down the block. Then it hit me that I'd never heard of meth being called "white." By the time I realized that, I was already at the suspect's door. I was feeling pretty nervous as this was my first undercover work, especially considering the circumstances of the case, so this revelation didn't help. I knocked on the door and a skinny, sickly looking white male came to the door, which had a window so we could see each other. He opened it slightly. By his look and demeanor, it was obvious I had the right house. He asked what I wanted, talking to me through the storm door. I told him I wanted some "white" and had been told he could hook me up. He looked me up and down for a second, then turned around and closed the door as he walked away. I didn't know that meant and I stood there for a few seconds, eventually realizing he wasn't intending to come back. As I walked back to the surveillance van, I felt quite upset. Well, I felt happy that I had failed at the "blowjob for discounted 8 balls" case because I never would have lived that down, but I was disappointed that I had failed at my first undercover work. More so, I was furious at my partner for the "white" thing. We were friends before the task force. Was she fucking with me? I like a good joke. Or did she want me to fail since I knew she wasn't thrilled to have another one of our Patrol Officers on the Task Force. I was wearing a surveillance wire listening device and all the support officers positioned in the area could hear the audio. As I walked back to the lead surveillance vehicle I said, "You better not motherfucking show your face to me for the rest of the day. White? White? You could have fucking gotten me killed with that shit!" For obvious reasons she avoided me the rest of the day, actually the rest of the week, which was a good thing because it allowed me to calm down. She was senior to me at Patrol, but only by a little. And she was senior to me at the Task Force, but that didn't mean much either. I decided to write it off as a joke or hazing and mended the working relationship the best I could, which remained strained during the rest of my time at the Task Force.

My second undercover situation went much smoother for me. Detective Teddy Strauch was working a case in Brooklyn Park and with a Confidential Informant (CI) who was willing to do a controlled buy, which meant we would make a purchase along with the C.I. and do the bust work later using warrants. I was the Undercover Officer again but this was much more in my comfort zone, partly because we were more in the "hood," closer to where I grew up. Plus it didn't involve a gay guy offering discounts for sexual favors. We used an undercover car and zigged and zagged through a large apartment complex until we found the target location. I was a little nervous because I knew my backup couldn't wiggle all the way back there without being seen by look outs so they had to stay a little farther back. Both the CI and I were white and this was predominantly a black residence complex. We were focused on buying crack cocaine since that was what was being sold at the location. Upon arrival, we were greeted by three black males as they surrounded the car. They were out of crack at the time and sold me a little marijuana. They offered to find some crack for me and worked on locating some. While waiting, they handed me a Budweiser beer. I HATE BEER! It is seriously foul tasting to me. But because of the circumstances, that was the best tasting beer I've ever had in my life!

The suspects said they had found a hook up for some crack cocaine on the north side of Minneapolis and wanted us to drive them over there. The north side of Minneapolis is where I grew up, but we were under a mandate at the Task Force to avoid that area because of some uprisings between Police and residents. I felt nervous as I came up with reasons not to go there, but they kept telling me I would be fine. Finally, I said with confidence, "Yo, I don't fuck with north side, they like to rip us white boys off!" They all started laughing and said, "Yeah, that's true!" One of the suspects brought me over to another apartment complex across the street. I followed him and another young male got into an elevator where he pushed the button for the top floor. We did the deal in the elevator. When we reached the bottom, he had me step back out. By doing so he prevented us from figuring out where to serve a search warrant.

After eight months of fantastic experience on the task force, we had staffing needs back on Patrol so I was transferred back to Patrol in February of 2003. I was a little sad but not too sad. I was more than confident that I had earned my way back when they had the next opening later that year. I had worked hard with lots of great cases and arrests and I had got some great experience. I was also engaged to be married that September so my fiancé was happy to know I would be shaved and cleaned up prior to the wedding. It was also nice to remember that there were more words in my vocabulary than fuck, shit, cock, pussy, and so on. When you work in the elements that we did, curse words become your primary language. I had also grown my hair and a half-assed beard to look more like a "doper," however my fiancé and mom weren't fond of the look. I looked like Shaggy from Scooby Doo, so that became my nickname on the task force.

I had fit the look well but it was great to finally clean up my hair and face when I ended my temporary stint and headed back to the Patrol Division.

When I returned to Patrol it was a pretty good feeling. I had only been gone for eight months so I wasn't too rusty. I had spent a lot of my downtime on the task force "ripping cars" (traffic stops) so I was ready to jump back into handling traffic violations. The best thing about being back on Patrol was the feeling that, regardless of the situation in front of me, I could handle it in an acceptable manner. I didn't feel like I knew everything, because I didn't and that is a dangerous way for a Police Officer to think. Instead, I felt I could find an acceptable resolution to most situations I came across.

What most people don't know about Law Enforcement is that we are judged and second guessed at practically EVERY action we take, and every decision we make or the lack thereof as well as timing and procedures. We are critiqued by everyone, including administrators, the news media, the public, street supervisors, and even our co-workers. Most people assume that police officers automatically have each other's backs. In reality, every action is scrutinized. And often the worst of the worst criticisms come from other officers. We are all guilty of constantly second guessing each other, especially if officers are on a different shift than you. Of course, in those situations, the person second guessing is almost never there and in your shoes, so it's stressful and obnoxious. The public constantly feel that police are wrong no matter what action they take. Then there is the media who love to sensationalize everything for a sizzling story. An experienced Law Enforcement Officer knows what I'm talking about. Of course that may be true for some other industries too, but most don't live in the glass house that law enforcement does. Our profession affects so many lives: the public, the officers, and even families. Always being under the proverbial microscope and seemingly never being right creates a significantly high level of stress. So it felt great to return to Patrol and feel so confident. And for the most part, that's exactly what occurred.

Well, except for one particular Sergeant. He was pretty calm and reasonable with me before my time at the Task Force, but since my return he was constantly on my ass and questioned almost everything I did. And I was pretty sure I knew why. He was dating that female Deputy who I had worked on the task force with and she and I butted heads A LOT. For the most part it seemed to be a case of mistrust between us. It started out with that move she did with my first undercover work and it seemed to escalate from there. Since there was always tension between us, my main task force partner Detective Pelkey and I often left her out of our cases unless we needed her help. We thought this would avoid the tension and conflict, but then she got suspicious and made a couple of cracks about why we were hiding things from her and were we doing illegal shit. I made it clear that she could review any of my case files to find out. In the end, neither of us were dealing with each other in the correct way but I'm sure she vented to her boyfriend who ended up being my shift Sergeant when I returned to street patrol. From day one of my return from the task force he seemed to take a special interest in me. Every traffic stop I was on, every call I was on, he always seemed to stop by. It was irritating at first, especially since I was one of the more experienced Deputies on the shift. Plus, Sergeants don't generally have enough time to focus on one Deputy.

As frustrating as it was I couldn't let it get to me. This is a part of the police world so I turned it into a little game. I would do a traffic stop and then time out how long it would usually take for him to swing by. Then I called out a couple of fake traffic stops on the radio and then hide around the corner and, sure enough, he rolled by shortly after. As soon as I saw him coming I would hit clear on my computer to clear the stop and tuck my squad out of view. There wasn't enough to keep a Sergeant up in Oak Grove and East Bethel, so it WAS NOT a coincidence. It became rather funny to me. I had shared this with a couple of my close partners on the department and we all got a good laugh out of it. One asked me if I was worried and suggested I file a union grievance. I wasn't interested in doing that. Besides, this was a much more fun way to deal with it. Eventually he backed off and began to trust me again.

I think he finally backed off when I had a pursuit in Linwood Township, located in the far north east tip of Anoka County where backup can easily be 20 plus minutes away. It was fast becoming an area where meth and meth labs were popping up with increased frequency. This meant it became my target city for enforcement. One day a small pickup truck crossed the center line and almost clipped me head on. As I turned my squad around he sped up and it was obvious he was trying to get away from me. I put my lights and siren on and after about half a mile he didn't respond. It was officially a pursuit and I notified dispatch. We were out pretty far in the county and the pursuit headed north to the county line, so I knew my chances of my backup assisting were limited, and there were never usually many officers on duty in the border counties to the north and east. I continued the pursuit ensuring I communicated every piece of information about the pursuit, including speeds, traffic in the area, and the direction and behavior of the officer. This same Sergeant was the supervisor on and, although he had backed off of me recently, I knew the likelihood of him judging me and calling off the pursuit were high if I wasn't absolutely clear with details.

The driver was moving around inside the vehicle a lot and kept lifting an item that was either a gun or a large blade. At one point, he tossed a bunch of papers and other items out of the pickup truck window. Deputy Chris Beck was a School Resource Officer at a school in Linwood and happened to be there, making him pretty close, so he was headed my way. This was good because Isanti County, Chisago County, and State Patrol were all tied up and not available to assist. As we went into the next county, Isanti County, the suspect turned into a farm driveway. I wasn't sure where I was, but I knew I was off of 261st Street. When I turned into that farmhouse driveway, I called out over the radio, "2Z36, he's turning south into a long driveway...tan house...lots of trees lining the driveway....he bailed...foot pursuit!" He jumped out of the moving vehicle, which looked to me like it then crashed into their house. As I began to chase him on foot I heard the homeowners yelling at the guy, "I'm gonna kick your ass!" As I got closer to him, a dog ran next to me barking. As a dog lover, I told the dog, "Go get 'em boy!" And he only obeyed! A second dog then ran next to me barking aggressively. I was later told by the dog's owner that I was lucky he didn't bite me. I said the same thing to the aggressive dog, "Go get 'em boy!" I couldn't believe my luck as the dog chased after him too. Neither of the dogs bit him, but they slowed him down enough for me to get within ten feet of him. I was about to shoot him with my Taser when I saw a four wheeler ATV speeding towards us from a different angle. It was the homeowner! By the direction and the speed the ATV was going, I thought it was going to hit the suspect. But fortunately for the suspect, he stopped and got down on the ground. With my Taser out I covered the suspect and told the homeowner to go to the street and wave my partner in since he might not know exactly where I am.

While waiting for my backup, who I knew was close by, I started to try to handcuff the suspect. He knew we were alone and resisted before I could get my cuffs out. He then started to resist more actively and fight me to get his hands back. I attempted to subdue him by deploying my Taser probes, but the Taser unit malfunctioned. I tried a couple more trigger pulls with no luck. The suspect must have heard me mumble about the Taser being a piece of shit as he then started to resist even more, trying to pull away from me. The Taser units also work as a touch Taser. I zapped him a couple of times but he squirmed away. During that time I retrieved my extra Taser cartridge and reloaded it and then backed up and deployed the prongs hitting him. It was fairly effective but he was still trying to fight, which is not uncommon if someone is high on drugs. I was pretty tired from chasing him and trying to fight him. As I was about to give him another round of shock, out of nowhere came Deputy Beck or, as I call him after that day, "Super Beck." Why? Because he always seemed to come out of nowhere. He flew through the air and landed right on the guy's back, all 260 pounds. I think I heard every ounce of air come out of that guy's lungs. It was good timing too, because I was exhausted and it turned out the suspect was extremely high on methamphetamine. I later heard from a toxicologist friend at the Bureau of Criminal Apprehension, who processed the suspect's blood for drugs and alcohol, that it was one of the highest readings of Meth from a blood sample that she had ever processed. After he was successfully taken into custody, we realized that the pickup truck, which had been recently "painted," was used a short time ago in a local burglary (thus the new "paint" job). And when I say "painted" I mean that after the burglary, he spray painted the pickup and over-sprayed half of the stolen items he still had in the back of the pickup truck. That essentially made the stolen items unsellable or at least of little value for him. He also had all the components for setting up a meth lab in the back of the truck. Inside, that large object I kept seeing him lift up, turned out to be a large machete.

My Sergeant arrived at the scene, which was a standard procedure after a pursuit, especially with the damage sustained when the suspect jumped out of his truck and it hit the house and other items. He asked me a couple details and said, "Good job Dustin, I think you got this." I was a little shocked, but pleased. After that day, he didn't make any more unnecessary visits to my traffic stops and there was no more second guessing. After that we had a great working relationship and we became friends again.

CHAPTER 4
MY GUN CULTURE

As police officers, we obviously train a lot in firearm use. For the Anoka County Sheriff's Office it was four times a year, which usually included regular range days, a night shoot, and a "shoot/no shoot" interactive virtual training. Personally, I believe we could do with more training with firearms but they do provide "open shoots," which are opportunities to go to the gun range and practice or catch up if you missed a previous firearms training. For me the gun range was all business. Some guys like to hang around the gun range and socialize after the shoot qualifying, but not me. I would go in, qualify the shoot, and head right out. I wouldn't even clean my gun there as I handled that at home. I would gladly meet people afterwards somewhere else, but my philosophy was to keep the social and fun out of my subconscious when it came to shooting scenarios.

Growing up, I wasn't exposed to a lot of firearms per se, at least not a lot of shooting of guns. My grandfather was an avid duck hunter and an active member of Duck's Unlimited, but I didn't get into that personally, and my father wasn't a big part of it either. When I was 8 or 9 years old my stepdad taught me to shoot a 22 rifle for the first time when we were at a cabin up north, but that was about as far as my gun exposure went up until that point. As he was a retired

Customs Agent, he did have guns around the house, which weren't stored in the safest or smartest way. The rules and education were quite different than compared to now, so I had plenty of moments of accessing his guns and I "played" with them. During my high school years I would show off the hand gun he kept in the night stand to my friends when they came to the house. I would show my friends his Uzi and SKS rifles when he was gone and I'm not even sure he was aware I knew he owned them. But my friends and I kept those secret gun moments in the house and unfired. Even with that, what we did was pretty stupid and unsafe.

I hadn't had much experience to gun exposure outside the house. Growing up on the north side of Minneapolis I remember a time where I was playing at the park across the street from the Jerry Gamble Boys Club. A kid had told the boys club staff about some other kids, all teenagers, climbing on the roof. They went after the kid that told and they ran by just feet from me with the kid pulling a black handgun out and pointing it at the group. It was a revolver, and probably a 38 special, but I'm not totally sure. Like an idiot, I simply stood there in amazement. He didn't end up pulling the trigger and they beat him up good. But those are the stories that tend to end with an innocent bystander being shot. Thank goodness that wasn't the outcome for me.

I remember one time in high school a close friend of mine was being badly bullied by another student, an upper classman who was a jerk. By this time we had moved to Minnetonka and were at Minnetonka Senior High. One day, my friend came up to me and said, "Hey, I need to show you something." He had a serious look on his face and I was both curious and concerned. We were in wood shop at the time and I followed him to a secluded storage area. I asked him what was up and suddenly he pulled out a handgun that had been concealed in his pants. I was shocked to say the least. "What the fuck are you doing?" I asked and I made him stuff it back out of view. It was a .357 revolver and he told me it was his dad's. Holy Hannah, I couldn't believe we were sitting there looking at a handgun… in school of all places. He claimed it was for protection because he was tired of being bullied. I wasn't confident that protection was his only reason and motivation. Either way, I didn't want him to get into trouble, or worse, do something stupid. I talked him into letting me hold on to it until after school and I told him I would keep it safe. I put it in my pants, hid it under my shirt, and snuck out of class and went to my locker. I hid it in there for safekeeping for the rest of the day, feeling nervous about it for the whole day. Luckily there weren't any problems. He and I often hung out after school so we drove to his house where I gave it back to him. Thankfully he didn't do anything that would have ruined his life. And thankfully I didn't get caught "helping" him. I realized later in life that my "helping" could have cost me my future career in Law Enforcement. He never brought it into school again, or at least he never told me if he did.

One of the most common questions Police Officers are asked, especially from children, is "Have you ever shot anyone?" The reality is, not many Police Officers will ever have to shoot their gun in the line of duty. There is a great deal of administrative and political chaos that can follow a shooting. Over my career I used my gun a few times, but generally only for dispatching injured animals or when covering high risk situations, but never pulling the trigger. One close call that sticks with me was a 911 call about two brothers fighting in the City of Ham Lake. I was the senior deputy on that call and had only been on my own a couple of years but had a new trainee riding with me. I wanted to wait for more backup for the call but it was busy at that moment and there were two of us, so it was time to carry on. We were sitting outside of the door listening and it was obvious that things were getting violent inside. We went around to the back door and heard someone say, "I'm going to kill you." That was the cue that we couldn't wait any longer. We entered guns drawn and found two males in the kitchen. There were two very large men, in height and width, in the kitchen. One of them was sitting with a very bloody face at the table. Blood was dripping badly from his face. The other was leaning against the sink area and he turned out to be the main suspect. He looked at me and asked, "What are you going to do, shoot me? You ain't gonna shoot me," and he started coming at me aggressively. He was so large he could have squashed me in a heartbeat. As I ordered him to stop several times, he ignored me and I moved my finger onto my trigger and resolved that I was going to have to shoot him. We were in very close quarters, there was nowhere to retreat to, and we didn't have things like Tasers at the time. Even though my finger was about to squeeze the trigger, I stopped myself. Physiologically people tend to experience "tunnel vision" during tense situations and have a hard time taking in the whole picture. I somehow got through the tunnel vision and found a last attempt at a resolution. I boot kicked him as hard as I could in the chest and he stumbled backwards. He stopped for a second and then gave up, putting his hands behind his back. He was taken into custody without further problems. On the way to jail he was very talkative and said, "You didn't hurt me, you know?! You just gave me gas so I gave up." I told him my next move would have been a bullet in the chest to which he replied, "Well, I'm glad that didn't happen." We both laughed and he was calm for the rest of the ride. And as odd as that was, even odder was my Captain pulling me aside the next day to thank me for not shooting him. "Um, okay Captain…you're welcome I guess." During my career there were other moments where I was close to pulling the trigger but found alternative options. This isn't easy to do when you only have seconds to decide but I'm glad I found a way.

Besides a couple of suicidal individuals with guns, my first true gun experience was on July 17, 2001, a full on active shooter situation. That day I had just arrived at the Patrol Station and we were getting ready for roll call when I heard a records tech hang up a phone and yell, "Officer down in Columbia Heights!" Deputy Mick Hlavinka and I were the two County Wide squads that day and both happened to have arrived a little earlier than usual. We ran to the Sergeant's office while he was on the phone. We were told to grab squads and head down there. Deputy Hlavinka and I headed to Columbia Heights as fast as we could. It was a sweltering day and the start of rush hour so, even with our emergency lights and sirens on, there was a lot of stop and go and braking. On the way we listened to the radio traffic and learned that Columbia Heights Officer McGee had been ambushed walking home from his Police Department. We didn't know his status, but we knew he had been shot several times and was holed up in a neighbor's house. The assailant had shot several rounds into the neighbor's house and then went to McGee's house and shot it up, where his daughter and her friend, who was the daughter of a prominent local judge, were hiding. Area agencies that were closer than us arrived before us, many of which were Minneapolis PD since they were a bordering city. I could hear gun fire over the various transmissions on the police radio and then we heard that two more officers had been shot. It sounded like a war zone over the radio.

As we approached the scene someone waved us down and told me my brakes were on fire. I assumed they were smoking from the constant braking. When I reached the next block and got out, I could see both Deputy Hlavinka's and my brakes were on fire. We had to head in on foot from there, so I popped the trunk, grabbed a fire extinguisher, and tossed it to a Community Service Officer who was directing traffic away from the shooter. As I was running I told him to put the fire out. Shortly after that, Deputy Hlavinka and I were nervously running up the block nearing the scene of the active shooter. That's when we heard that the suspect had been shot and was in custody. As we approached I saw that Minneapolis Police had the suspect in custody. He was shirtless and I noticed a couple of red spots that were obviously gunshots. It turned out that one of Minneapolis Police Officers had shot him with a shotgun. I spent the next few hours helping on scene with evidence processing. The vast amount of rounds I helped mark, and seeing all of the bullet holes was a real eye opener. The crime scene spanned over several blocks. I'm not sure I ever processed the stress of that shooting, but I think it helped me years later when it came to my own shooting. Officer McGee eventually healed and returned to work, and the suspect, David Byrne, was found to be mentally ill and not competent to stand trial but he was committed to a mental hospital. He claimed that Officer McGee was sneaking into his house at night through the wires and speakers. Interestingly, David Byrne had murdered his wife decades before and had already served that jail time.

To this day I still own firearms and I probably will for the rest of my life. I don't go to the range as much but at least a couple of times a year I do a retired officer shoot qualification and a general range day. And I carry my gun often, especially with the crazy world that seems to be going on around us these days. I hope to never have to use the gun again, but I also hope to never be in a situation where I need a gun and don't have it.

CHAPTER 5
OFFICER DOWN

My birthday is on May 14 and as I approached my thirty-first birthday, I was preparing to remodel my bathroom. I was scheduled for my normal three days off so I took a couple of extra days of vacation. I gutted the bathroom that week so I could re-tile and put a new tub in. On May 12, I was scheduled for a County Wide Night Power Rover squad. Night Power meant that I worked from 7 p.m. to 3:30 a.m. I loved Night Power shifts because they are in the core of the action. County Wide Rover was a rare shift, especially night power. That meant we had plenty of squads on. Rover squads aren't assigned to any specific area and generally float around covering calls when others are tied up on calls or on their dinner break. Other than that, it's complete freedom. For me that meant targeting Drug Houses because that's how I roll!

Deputy Samantha (Sam) Cruze was also working a County Wide Rover Squad that night, so we were really overstaffed. Sam was a Community Service Officer (CSO) for my department for the two years prior to being hired as a full-time Deputy. She was a great CSO, hardworking and smart. We were friends and I enjoyed her being a part of the department. I was pleased when she was hired on as a full-time Deputy. During her third phase of FTO training she worked with Deputy Gerry Dubay. Deputy Dubay and I were friends and worked the same shift, often on the same calls, which meant Sam was on many calls with me too. I did all I could to test the new Deputies out, forcing them to make decisions about calls they weren't as experienced with as part of their training process. Sam was no different, except she accepted every challenge I presented her with and her resolutions were spot on each time in my eyes. If nothing else, her resolutions were always acceptable decisions.

The night I was scheduled for the Night Power Rover shift, Sam had just finished her FTO Training and was two days on her own. Prior to that shift Sam told me she wanted to learn about working drug interdiction and targeting meth houses. I was more than happy to oblige and thought she would be good at it. Since we were both scheduled as Night Power Rovers on May 12, that was the perfect time. So that was the plan. But plans are sometimes altered. Before my shift that day I got a page from Sergeant Plattner asking if I would be willing to switch shifts because both the Night Power Andover Deputy and the C Shift Andover Deputies had taken sick days. I was disappointed but wasn't too surprised. We work very long hours and stressful shifts so when there are that many squads on duty often Deputies use a sick day as a personal day to reset. Sergeant Plattner wanted to know if I was willing to switch to C Shift. I felt bad but I declined because I was off for the next five days and didn't want to start the days with no sleep. Plus, I hated working C Shifts, especially in Andover. C Shift is boring enough to work, but Andover is even worse and filled with barking dog calls, speeding complaints, neighbor disputes, and domestic disputes. *Nothing ever happens in Andover!* Oh, how I would eventually regret making that statement!

Sam took the Andover Night Power Shift, so she was assigned as call sign 4A57. I'm not sure why they didn't want to put her on the Andover C Shift. I'm guessing it was because she had been two days on her own, but I am more than confident she would have handled it fine. I worked a Night Power shift and County Wide Rover for the first half of the shift. At 10:30 p.m. I switched over to be the first half of Andover C Shift as 3A40. Sam and I met after roll call but I told her I knew of no active drug houses in Andover at the time and I would probably do a lot of traffic stops to see what I could dig up. The first part of the shift was relatively uneventful for the most part. Just before 2 a.m. I was headed to get a soda when I passed a car that had obviously illegal tint. I recognized the car and knew he had been warned and ticketed before, and the owner was known as a weed smoker and possibly more. I did a traffic stop and was doing some checks on him when Sam stopped by to check on me. I told her I would be all right. Then she got another call about loud music at 2118 140th Lane NW, one house west of the caller's address. Shortly after Dispatch checked my status and I said I would be clear and in the area of Sam's call since it was right around the corner.

My traffic stop was about five or five blocks away from her call so I arrived within a minute. Sam had driven past the caller's address with her window open to see if she could hear the music and then turned around and came back, pulling up to the address as I pulled up across the street. My squad was on 140th Lane NW on the north side of the road,

46

facing west. Sam's squad was on the south side of the road, the same side as the caller's and suspect's house. The caller's house was the east end of her duplex and shared a driveway with another duplex that was unattached on the east side of the driveway. When we exited our squads the original complainant was taking out her garbage at 2118 140th Lane NW and had approached Sam. I didn't hear the conversation very well as I let Sam take the lead. At that point we were at the end of the shared driveway and I could hear music coming from 2110 140th Lane NW. There were two vehicles in the driveway. One was a white passenger car in front of the garage, and on the side of the garage was an SUV, which looked inoperable. There were no cars in the street and no lights on in the front area inside the duplex, so it didn't look like a party. Sam said the complainant had said since she called the music had been turned down a little, but it was still pretty loud.

The loud music house was the west side of the duplex, which was the right side as we looked at it, and left of the caller's address. There were two or three small trees in the front yard but I didn't even register them. The front door had a storm door and there was a picture window to the right of the door with four sections. There was a full moon that night. As we approached, Sam looked at me and I said, "I'm your backup, it's your call." As we approached closer the music was louder and it was clearly a Bee Gees disco song. Normally this isn't the type of loud music we are used to dealing with. Sam and I did a little dance as we approached. As we neared the door, Sam stepped up on the concrete steps and landed in front of the door. I stood in front of the windows peeking inside. I told Sam that it was dark inside but there was a light on in a back room to the right, possibly a kitchen area. Even though it was dark inside, the moonlight lit up the front room, which appeared to be a living room.

Sam rang the doorbell a couple of times. After the second ring I noticed a shadow move in the far lighted room and a white male stepped out of the back room, paused, and then went back inside. I told Sam and by the time she looked in the window the male returned to the front room. He was a white male, tall looking, with blonde or light brown hair in a short buzz cut. Only this time he had a gun in his hand. I don't recall which hand it was, but at that moment it seemed like the biggest gun I had ever seen. Not so much because it was physically large, although it was a Sig Sauer 45 Caliber, but because of the situation. He was holding the gun down at a low ready angle. I started to duck and looked at Sam and said, "Holy shit, he's got a…" At that moment I heard Sam yell "GUN." I drew my handgun from my holster as did she. We were both carrying our agency issued Beretta 9mm semi-automatic hand guns. I'm right handed and so as I was drawing my gun, my body leaned to the left and my momentum carried me that way. I went with it and continued in that direction. It was the same direction as Sam had jumped off of the steps so we were both on the left side of the door a few feet away.

My back was against the wall halfway between the two halves of the duplex. Sam was on my right and the door was on my left. I quickly scanned the area but saw no real cover nearby. Apparently I had chosen the wrong direction to go when I went with my momentum and we were both sitting ducks. The trees in the yard weren't big enough to provide any real cover and the closest squad was across the street. The other corner of the duplex was a possibility but by this time I could hear that the front door had been opened and I could now see the storm door slowly opening, and I didn't feel like being shot in the back. Sam and I both started yelling commands pretty loudly. "Sheriff's Office, Sheriff's Office, drop the gun" came out of my mouth several times. Sam yelled something similar in a higher pitched voice. I realized if he started shooting at us we would both probably get hit, so I stepped out into the yard to separate us. Unfortunately, that put me in his direct line of fire. I was pretty much committed at that point. With my gun low I continued angling into a position where I could at least see how big of a threat this really was.

As we both continued to yell commands, the whole time I was thinking, *There's no way this is going to happen.* Finally, I yelled, "It's the police. Drop the fucking gun!" By this time I was directly in front of the door, about eight feet away from the storm door. I saw the individual's shape. I still couldn't tell you what hand he held the gun in, but I could now see about half of his body. Most importantly, I could see he had raised the gun and it was pointed at my chest from an elevated position. My gun was already pointed at his torso area and in my mind I was mentally committed to pulling the trigger. By the time I put my finger on the trigger he had his gun pointed between my eyes. It looked like the biggest barrel I'd ever seen in my entire life. I felt like I could easily crawl inside of it. Time had slowed down to a crawl. Reflecting, it is amazing how fast it all went down as my mind raced. I processed an incredible amount of thoughts from beginning to end.

With the barrel of his gun still pointed at me, I pulled the trigger twice and heard a single loud "POP." I saw him flinch and he let out a strange grunt. I was confident I had hit him. Ironically at the point he retracted after my bullet struck him, his shadow oddly resembled the gun training silhouettes we use. Except silhouettes don't shoot back! I had my flashlight out and started running to the white car in the driveway for cover. I held the flashlight in my left hand and used that wrist to support my right hand, which had my hand gun in it to try to light up the front room as I ran for cover hoping to figure out where he was. Almost immediately I heard two more pops, and I felt a thud against the right side of my body. Both rounds came from the four panel picture window to the right of the door. The first one hit my right arm in the upper bicep area, spinning my body to the right. Everything went in slow motion. As I spun, it was similar to the movie *The Matrix* when everything goes in slow motion. As I was spinning my gun went flying into the yard. I remember thinking to myself, *Holy shit I just got shot.* It felt surreal and I remember thinking I must be sleeping, and this was just a dream. Then the second round hit me in my mid pelvic area. Neither shot hurt, but the second one dropped me on the spot. I let out a strange high pitch cackle, which I don't think I could ever recreate, and I never want to, that's for sure. Sam tells me it was a haunting sound.

I didn't feel it in my pelvic region, but in my right groin area. When I hit the ground I was amazed at my ability to think and assess the situation. Time sped up to normal speed and

I still didn't feel any pain. I was probably about five to ten feet from the center of the front windows. I looked around for my gun but I couldn't see it. Assessing my right arm, it was obviously broken. I could tell my mid humorous bone had been completely severed. I wiggled my right hand fingers and noticed them moving, which was good. I started crawling towards the white car in the driveway. The shock of the "double tap" was starting to affect my body and energy. I finally reached the rear driver's side wheel when my body started to give way. Actually, it may have been my mind giving way at that moment. I felt like I couldn't crawl anymore and I collapsed flat. I laid there for a couple of seconds breathing and trying to figure out what I should do – what I could do. I was still close to the window and scared he was going to shoot me again. My right groin area continued to feel strange and I felt positive that the bullet must have severed or cut my femoral artery. All my First Responder training had taught me that there is a serious risk of bleeding to death if the femoral artery is cut or torn. I needed to let someone know right away. I grabbed my right hand (broken arm) and forced it across my chest to my shoulder. My radio mic was clipped to my left side shoulder strap. I tried to get out on the radio a couple of times with no success. I raised my radio as high as I could with my left hand but still couldn't get out. I'm not sure if it was all the other radio traffic, a bad signal or if my radio was damaged. I got pissed at that point and threw it.

All I could do at that moment was wait for the cavalry to come and save me. I put my left hand over the area on my right groin where I felt the weird sensation and the general area of the femoral artery. I was face down and I tried to apply pressure and did some breathing exercises to slow down my heart rate. My hope was to limit any excess bleeding until help arrived. The unfortunate part about breathing and relaxing is that my adrenaline started to dump and I started to feel the pain in my arm now. It hurt fiercely! I was still worried the suspect was going to come back and shoot me again so I lay there pretending to be dead. I could hear Sam talking to me, telling me she was still there and watching over me. I didn't know exactly where she was, but I knew she was close by. I couldn't answer because I didn't want to give away that I was alive. I later found out from Sam that she thought I was dead and continued to talk to me "just in case." I really appreciated that because it kept me a bit calmer knowing I wasn't there alone. And she was risking her own life to calm someone down who she thought was dead.

As I laid there the first thing that flashed through my mind was my 6-year-old son, Jacob, the light of my life. My brother died when his kids were 3 years old and 9 months old and I didn't want my son growing up without a father like they had to. I tried to remain calm. I remembered in Law Enforcement Skills training, our instructor Bob Penney, a Champlin PD Officer, would have us run laps yelling, "If I am shot, I will survive....if I am stabbed, I will survive." So lying there, breathing calmly and silently to myself, I kept repeating those very words. "If I am shot, I will survive....if I am shot, I will survive". I heard squads screaming to the area but I couldn't tell how far away they were. Suddenly over the radio, I heard Dispatch call to 4Z13, which was Sergeant

Plattner, who had arrived somewhere in the area. After he acknowledged, Dispatch said:

"At 2110 140th Lane we have a 911 open line. They said someone had been shot and that somebody was barely breathing. Person was making a moaning noise inside the location. We believe it's related."

At that moment I knew the guy was either dead or dying and no longer able to shoot me. I can't tell you exactly how I knew, but I just knew. It was such a relief. But with that sense of relief came a bigger adrenaline dump and another wave of intense pain. I heard Sam and Sergeant Plattner over the radio coordinating getting him to her position. I heard Sergeant Plattner shortly after that somewhere nearby making a tactical plan for extraction, which is the standard way to handle such a situation to make sure they could get to me while protecting both me and themselves. I was hurting pretty badly at that point and still convinced I was bleeding to death. I yelled out a couple of times to make sure they knew where I was. "I'm over here…I've been shot…get me out of here." Suddenly I heard footsteps running up to me and I heard, "Dustin…it's Scott Nolan. Do you know who I am?" I told him yes and to get me out of there. Scott Nolan was a Sergeant with nearby Anoka Police Department, and known to be a little off his rocker. Not in a bad way though, and I'm not at all surprised he bypassed the tactical approach and ran up to me. That's why he's known as a little crazy!

Sergeant Nolan immediately checked my visible back for blood and wounds. I told him I had been shot in the right bicep and my right groin and that I was bleeding to death and in an immense amount of pain. Then I heard another person running up to me, who I later determined to be Sergeant Urquhart from Coon Rapids Police Department, followed by a whole bunch of other Officers. I looked up at one point and I saw a wall of brown and blue between the window I was shot through and myself. Each and every one of those officers had put their lives on the line for me. What a bunch of heroes! As I shed a tear, I can never express enough of my appreciation to their dedication, including those who I didn't name.

The ambulance was caught a block down because of all of the squads so they were going to carry me on a backboard. I was face down and my left shoulder was nearly up against the tire of the car. I heard them talk about having to roll me onto my right arm. By this time, I was in so much pain I would have none of that. I grabbed my right arm and pinned it to my chest rolled up onto my left arm, and I yelled out, "Fuck that, put the backboard behind me." I think they were shocked but I couldn't handle the pain much longer and wanted nothing to do with rolling onto the broken arm. They got me secured and several officers carried me on the backboard down the street to the ambulance. It was about a block away because in the chaos of the arriving squads, the ambulance couldn't get through. I remember lying on the ground thinking I didn't know if the pain could get any worse. Well, I was wrong. When they were carrying me, one officer's hip kept smacking into my broken arm, which certainly trumped the pain I had previously experienced. I screamed out several times begging to make it stop. I nearly passed out from the pain. In no way do I blame him though.

When we reached the ambulance I asked Sergeant Nolan to ride with me. I felt pretty vulnerable at that point plus I wanted to make sure details got out in case it was a lethal wound. I knew one of the paramedics. She looked at me and said, "Dustin, I was hoping it wasn't you." I responded with something like, "Well, Theresa, I'm glad it's you who's picking me up." I meant it in a fun and flirty way, which my partners later said made them feel better because that was "normal Dustin." I also meant it because it was a familiar face helping me. She wasted no time in getting us out of there. She even took off before the squads could setup an escort. Often, when a police officer is shot, other officers will escort the ambulance to help it get through intersections faster and safer. Again, I was glad to be out of there and on the way to the hospital. I gave Sergeant Nolan a rundown of what had happened and a description. The paramedic and Sergeant Nolan were talking about getting my bullet proof vest off. I remember hearing him saying, "Don't cut it. Let's see if we can get it off without that. I remember I got mad because I couldn't handle much more pain. I started saying, "Just cut the fucking thing off." Somehow they got it off without cutting it and causing additional pain.

I'm not for medication of any sort, but at that point I was literally begging for something to help the pain. My adrenaline was fading by now and the pain was tremendous. I was given something on the way to the hospital, which took the edge off the pain. Being a Drug Recognition Expert (DRE) and previously certified as an Emergency Medical

Technician (EMT), I understood emergency medical procedures and the importance of certain vital signs, so I was listening to my vitals. I asked them to repeat them and my pulse was elevated but okay, and my blood pressure was also elevated but in the acceptable range. I asked how bad my leg was bleeding and they said, "Not much at all." I looked at my right hand and checked if I could wiggle the fingers. They still worked. I knew my arm was broken but at least it appeared to be functional. Then I thought to myself, well I may have said it out loud too, "*I JUST SURVIVED A FUCKING SHOOTING!"*

CHAPTER 6
WHAT'S UP DOC?!

Based on the nature of my injuries, they ordered Life Link, which is a medical chopper, to take me to a trauma center. Life Link happened to be in Brainerd, which is a forty-five minute flight, but was redirected and on the way back to the area. Because of that they transported me by ambulance to Mercy Hospital in Coon Rapids first to make sure I was stable. It was a short ride to the hospital and a whole medical team was ready to go. I was in a lot of pain, but felt good as I realized I had survived being shot twice. The doctors immediately started to cut my clothes off. As they cut my pants off, I bellowed out, "Just so you know ladies, I've been shot so I probably have shrinkage!" That got a little chuckle out of a few of them, and for me it was an outlet for my silly personality. At least I hadn't lost my sense of humor. Later, when talking to my family, friends and partners, the common theme was hearing the joking like that meant that I was going to be okay.

I was on an emotional roller coaster after that point with fear, anger, pain, and happiness, all rearing their weary heads. When my pants and underwear had finally been cut off, all my humor ended for a while. I saw the eyes of one of the nurses widen as she looked at my pelvic region, so I looked down. And that's when I realized I hadn't been hit in the groin area, but right above the base of my penis. 1/8th of an inch above! I went ballistic, flailing around and cursing. "That motherfucker just about shot my dick off," I said, followed by several uses of the F word and others. There was a tremendous amount of fear coursing through me. At one point I was in mid curse word "Mother-fu..." when everything went black. I assume they put something in my IV to put me out, and not for the last time.

It happened again when they were wrapping my right arm. There was a perfect round shaped hole, about the 45 caliber bullet size, in my bicep. I was on lots of pain meds at that point so I was quite loopy and the bullet hole intrigued me. I insisted someone take a picture of it for investigatory and personal reasons. They kept saying that would happen later and I had an outburst about that too, and again found myself blacking out mid curse word.

Mercy E.R. Doctors stabilized me until the Life Link helicopter arrived. They rolled me out to the chopper and loaded me in. It was manned with two people – a pilot and a Flight Nurse. We flew en route to North Memorial Medical Center in Robbinsdale, just outside of the north side of Minneapolis where I grew up and was a Level 1 Trauma Center. Mid-flight I was feeling okay as I knew my vitals were good and it was obvious the bullet had missed my femoral artery. My arm was broken but the nerves seemed to be intact since I could move my hands and fingers. And I was on a good dose of pain meds to keep the pain manageable. I kept looking up to look out of the window. I mean, how many times would I get the opportunity to see the Minneapolis Skyline from a helicopter ride? The Flight Nurse kept telling me to lie back and I kept saying I was fine and wanted to see. We got into a little argument about it. I looked at him angrily and said, "Motherfucker, I just survived a shooting. I've earned...." And YES, you guessed it, I blacked out again. I don't take it personally though and I felt pretty bad about it afterwards. Later I went to the hospital to thank the staff, and I sent letters to Life Link apologizing for my outbursts and thanking all of them for their hard work.

By the time we arrived at North Memorial Hospital I had settled down quite a bit. They brought me into the E.R. and removed a 45 caliber bullet from my right thigh, just below the buttock. It was lodged about half an inch under my skin and I could physically see the bump and feel it through the skin with my hand. It had travelled from the entry point just above the base of my penis through my groin area and lodged into my right thigh below the buttock. The Commander, Loni Payne, was there at the time and another Deputy, and they remained in the emergency room. I didn't work much with the Commander since she was in charge of the Criminal Investigative Division, but I enjoyed our interactions. She had a calming nature and we cracked jokes and laughed together. I have always used humor to help me through difficult situations.

After they removed the bullet, they put me in a semi-private room in the E.R. and were planning to take me to surgery soon. The answer always seemed to be, "In about 45 minutes." I was soooooo thirsty at that point, and the hospital only gave me a few ice chips. The SWAT team came to see me and we had a few good chuckles. As good as it was to see my brothers, I could see how relieved they were to see me alive and cracking jokes. I think the smiles all went away, at least for a couple of moments, when I told them he almost shot my penis off. But the smiles eventually returned. I told them I knew I had shot him and asked if he was dead or alive. They hesitated as they all glanced at each other, but one of them told me the guy was dead, likely as a result of my bullet. I'm not sure if I had any feelings about it right then. I think I was on too much of a high from surviving the shooting and I was on quite a bit of pain medication. But I felt relieved he wasn't going to come after me for revenge and that he wasn't at the same hospital, which often happens in these situations.

One SWAT member in particular was Deputy Chris Beck, among many close friends of mine. I finally told Deputy Beck that I was dying of thirst and NEEDED a Coca Cola...NOW!!!! Deputy Beck didn't hesitate to go get me that Coca Cola and snuck it into me. That was much appreciated. The nurse caught me with the contraband Cola shortly after and took it away before I could drink much of it. She took it, but then said, "It looks like it's going to be a few hours before your surgery, so take one last sip." God bless her! Shortly after that, while the SWAT team was visiting me, Sheriff Bruce Andersohn, the Sheriff of my county, stopped by. We were closer when he was a Captain of our Patrol Division and he was a great Captain. As a Sheriff, let's just say there was a difference in opinion about him by many of us once he got the number one spot. He was a hammer-fisted leader who seemed to only want things done his way and if you didn't follow that direction, it sure seemed like he was coming after you for messing with his vision of the department. As a Captain, his common saying was "if you want to make mayonnaise, you have to crack a couple of eggs". Not so much when he became Sheriff. He seemed far more concerned about his public image than he was about his officers. He went from being respected as a Captain to hated by many of his officers, especially after the shooting. That being said, I appreciated him stopping by to check on me. I was pretty doped up with pain meds at that point. I made a joke about one of the senior guys that "he was just mad because I got one before he did." The Sheriff didn't find that funny at all, and he looked angry and stormed out. I admit it was an inappropriate joke, but I was extremely doped up. While I was out on that early Medical Leave, it was the last time I saw or heard from him personally.

I had quite a few visitors in that E.R. but I don't remember a lot of them. I felt exhausted and on pain meds. But each visit still meant a lot to me. I do remember the positive feeling I got every time I saw a new face. I woke up in a private room. At around 6:00 a.m. Crime Lab Sergeant Kreyer came to take some pictures of my wounds and to "take blood." This is an important part of these investigations to ensure I wasn't on any chemicals or intoxicants, such as drugs or alcohol. Although I had nothing to hide, I remember feeling a little anxious. My union steward wasn't there yet and I didn't know what I should and shouldn't do. Also, I think the pain meds were increasing my anxiousness. I told him I wanted to talk to my union steward first and asked if he should be present. Sergeant Kreyer was only doing his job and I could see he was also in an awkward place. In the end I agreed to it before the union steward arrived. Sergeant Kreyer was professional and I had nothing in my system anyway, but that didn't take away from my apprehension.

While I was at the hospital, for the first couple of days or so, there was always an armed Deputy with me, which was comforting since I would often wake up unsure of where I was or what was going on. My mom showed up at some point, which was also a relief. I'm no momma's boy, but my mom and I have a great relationship and connection, especially since the death of my brother ten years before. She came into my room and hugged me, and I started crying, along with her. I said, "I'm so sorry, Mom." She looked confused and asked me why I was sorry. I reminded her, "I promised you I'd always go home at the end of the shift and I broke that promise." My mom hugged me a little tighter and told me a hospital room was just like a hotel room, so it counts. Seeing my 6-year-old son was emotional too. He was the first thing that had gone through my mind the moment I thought I was going to die. My fiancé at the time had been picked up by a Deputy and driven there, so thankfully she was around fairly early on and ready to comfort me when needed.

Sam came to the hospital within the first few hours after my arrival. I don't remember at exactly what time, but I was glad to see her, both as my friend, and as my partner in the shooting. I knew she was okay, but for some reason I needed to see it for myself. She came in looking exhausted and emotional, almost nervous. I had never seen Sam like that before. I asked everyone else to leave the room so we could talk. By reading the case file, I later learned that she had been instructed not to talk to me about the case. I understand why since they hadn't yet received my statement, but I needed to piece all this together emotionally. Sam was standing there nervously looking at me, obviously exhausted, with her head down. We both remained silent for what felt like forever. I asked her to come and sit on my bed and she did. I asked her bluntly, "Okay, so tell me what happened." Sam shared with me how things went down from her set of eyes and I accepted it without hesitation. It made sense to me. She said from her vantage point she couldn't fully see the man and she had only seen flashes of light. She said she knew I had fired my weapon and then the suspect had disappeared. She admitted she thought I was dead. Imagine after only two days working on your own, staring at what you think is your dead partner and friend. From that point forward, if anyone tried to say anything negative in front of me about Sam's actions during the shooting, I quickly laid into them. As far as I was concerned, it wasn't up to them to decipher the appropriateness of her actions because they weren't there. Unfortunately, I later learned how bad some of my partners and friends had treated her, both deputies and the administration.

By this time, I was on a self-administering morphine drip. I didn't take a lot, as I'm not a big fan of the feeling. I do have a fairly high pain tolerance and only used it when I absolutely needed it. The nurses scolded me and told me I should be using it more often so that when pain did come it would not be so hard to manage. So I hesitatingly kept it more consistent. As a DRE we learned that a Narcotic Analgesic, such as morphine, often causes a person to be "on the nod," which means they will pass out from the drug in short bursts, but often still hear the conversation going on. That is what happened to me. I would be in mid-conversation and then suddenly fall asleep, only to wake up five to fifteen minutes later and continue my conversation or story. And that makes sense, because oh how I love to tell stories!

That first morning after the shooting was strange. The incident was all over the news and they mentioned I was in surgery at that exact moment. That gave those of us in the room a good laugh because I sat in bed anxiously awaiting the same surgery the news said I was already having. Not so funny to me was when I watched the news conference and listened to the Sheriff, my boss, say, "We do know that officers really need to understand the principle that there's no such thing as a routine call."

I piped up, "What an ass!" It's more how he said it that bothered me. Any experienced officer knows there is no such thing as a routine call. I thought to myself, *Maybe he himself should be the one remembering that* and I flipped my middle finger at the TV.

They finally brought me into surgery later that morning. Dr. Kraft was my primary surgeon and he was a top notch orthopedic surgeon. Dr. Kraft reviewed the damage to my arm with me after the surgery. He started by making sure I noticed that when he made the nine-inch cut in my arm, he took care to protect my tattoo on the upper part of that arm. I was surprised at how long the cut was and I can't even tell you how many stitches I had. Before the shooting, I used to joke when telling stories by starting with, "So there I was." This battle scar certainly gave me the opportunity to tell a story that way, although ironically it took a decade to be able to inject much humor while telling it. Dr. Kraft went into great detail about my injury and the surgery. As I'm a "need to know" person, I really appreciated his explanations.

The bullet that hit me in my upper right arm, entered in the right bicep area and hit the bone. It deflected off the bone and exited through the back side of my arm on the inside. That bullet fell somewhere on the ground at the scene. It entered my arm a little higher than halfway between my elbow and my shoulder. Dr. Kraft said the shockwave from the 45 caliber stretched my radial nerve around like a rubber band. It destroyed about half of my bicep and half of my triceps. It completely blew out about one half to three quarters of my humorous bone, which is the upper bone in your arm. My arm was a mess. Dr. Kraft said the injury to the radial nerve was "the worst I've ever seen without actually being damaged." The injury to the radial nerve caused a loss of sensation in my arm, hand, and fingers, especially numbness in my right forearm. Since the bone had completely separated, the right humorous bone was repaired with an eight-inch plate and held by nine titanium screws screwed into the remaining bone. Dr. Kraft told me the bone would regenerate over the next year. Although the plate could be removed after the bone regenerated completely, he recommended leaving the plate in my arm permanently unless it started to bother me. The plate is very close to the radial nerve and removing the plate could damage the nerve, and removing it would be like drilling nine holes in a 2 x4 inch piece of wood, leaving it very susceptible to breaking until those holes healed. He warned me that the proximity of the plate to my radial nerve could cause pain and problems and to let him know if that happened. Long term, the nerve would gain sensation in the forearm, but even now I continue to suffer from issues of the plate and nerve. During the first year I suffered issues with my fine motor skills in the right arm and hands. I couldn't even push the quarters in the pay slots on a pool table. Although the severity of that faded, today I still have problems throwing a football or playing darts. Doing so gives me pain near my right elbow for two or three days. I wasn't fond of the idea of going back under the knife, so I've had to readjust my lifestyle to avoid the things that aggravate it.

Although a lot scarier, the overall damage from the shot to the pelvic region was less serious. The bullet travelled pretty cleanly from the entry point to where it finally lodged in my right thigh about half an inch below the skin. They removed that in the E.R. Over the next few days the right side testicle swelled to the size of my fist. There was discussion about having to remove my right testicle but fortunately the swelling went down and it returned to its normal size. It was tremendously painful, but there was no long term damage as evidenced by the birth of my other two youngest sons. However, I do have heightened sensitivity in that testicle and there is internal scar tissue. I learned that the hard way when I had a vasectomy.

I had lots of visitors during my stay at North Memorial and a huge amount of great support from family, friends, and other law enforcement. It was very humbling. The department paid a Deputy to stay with me twenty-four hours a day for the first few days. The officers and the hospital kept the media, snoopy people, and any upset family members of Eric Nylen, the suspect who had died. Although, for the record I do not believe any of them turned up to the hospital, but they needed to take precautions because it was a police shooting. I had just killed a member of their family and we had no idea how they might react. My mom even had to go to security and present her identification when she arrived. My Sheriff's administration decided to replace the armed Deputies after the third day with unlicensed Reserve Deputies without running it by me. Although that might sound okay, Reserve Deputies, although trained in some hand-to-hand combat, are not as well trained or armed as a full-time Deputy. Not to mention, not all of our reserves are the folks I want in my room. Don't get me wrong, I was also a reserve at one time, and I often had the reserves help on my calls so they had something to do. But I didn't want them guarding me, asking me about hypothetical police situations, and so on. My administration should have asked or at least advised me and gave me the opportunity to agree or disagree. I had a great relationship with many of the Reserve Deputies, but plenty of them drove me nuts and I didn't want to deal with that stress. I told Deputy Wiley, my union steward who informed me of the change, to tell the Undersheriff to cancel that crap idea. And guess what, in the next twenty-four to forty-eight hours I had a licensed Deputy by my side for almost twenty-four hours a day. It turns out the Deputies were upset about the situation too and several volunteered their time. I am truly honored and humbled by this gesture.

PART 2
The Gates of My Hell

CHAPTER 7
HOMECOMING

I was discharged from North Memorial Hospital after five days of being there. I was happy to come home also nervous. *Where am I going to sleep? How am I going to sleep? Do I have to worry about the suspect's family? Will my penis ever work again? Can I have more kids? Will I be a police officer again?* I had so many questions that only time could answer. I realized fast that sometimes the hardest things to deal with are those for which you have no answer and no control over.

No matter what, I was glad to be home. My sleeping arrangements were simple because I slept in my recliner. It was too difficult to get up by myself in my regular bed and it hurt to lie flat. So the recliner was a perfect solution. It was extra soft, and it even had a little refrigerator in the arm rest. Now if the recliner only would have had some kind of built in bathroom system I would have been in Heaven. The simplest tasks were quite challenging with only one functioning arm and hand, especially since I'm right handed and that was my injured arm. Above all the other difficulties, I quickly realized I was going to have to wipe my "you know what" with my left hand, which is a lot harder than you think. Eating left handed was quite a chore as well, but I tried not to let it get to me. I am a big hugger and it felt strange to give my fiancé and son one-handed, left armed hugs for but that's what I was stuck with and it was better than no hugs at all. And at least I was still around to hug and be hugged. Even showering was difficult. It felt strange at the age of 31 to ask my mom, who was there to help for a few days after I got out of the hospital, to help me shower, but that was the hand we were dealt with at the time.

The first month was tough. It didn't help that I was home all day with too much time to think. I was filled with a variety of emotions involving everything that was going on and had gone on. I had always been good at separating simultaneous stresses in my life but this one was tough. I had quickly started to develop a blurred feeling when it came to my emotions as I was pulled in so many directions. I was dealing with the physical pain obviously involved with my injuries. I was struggling with wanting to be independent, yet I couldn't even shower properly. I was dealing with the feeling of knowing someone had tried to kill me, and had nearly succeeded. I was starting to feel abandoned by the administration of my department. I had the fight of the investigators wanting an official statement and my attorney pushing them away, with me the one to negotiate both sides. It hurt to know I was sleeping separate from my fiancé. I wondered if my penis would ever work again and, if it did, whether I could have more children. We were already scheduled to get married later that fall and I wondered how well I was going to be healed for my wedding and honeymoon. I was dealing with the obnoxious personality of my work comp administrators at the county and how insensitive and pushy they were. And I was trying to still be a good fiancé and father during all of these confusing times. Not an easy set of tasks at all. I struggled with the curiosity of the unanswered questions and details about the shooting. And, there's one more thing I was dealing with, one thing I'm not sure I have ever dealt with…the taking of another man's life.

Overall, I wasn't concerned anymore about retribution from his family. Maybe a little, but not too much. I knew they were upset but the information filtering back to me indicated that there wasn't an obvious or threatening anger to be concerned about. I had my mom around me for a couple of days, my fiancé taking care of me, and many of my Anoka County Deputies and Blaine Officers stopping by the house. As exhausting as having guests was, it felt great to see and feel the support. Not to mention, I believe it was important for their own healing too. My law enforcement family mowed my lawn while I was in the hospital and a couple of times after that. My partners stopped in to share stories of the road and update me on general office stuff unrelated to my shooting. One reoccurring theme that impressed me was how my incident seemed to have brought the community closer and more connected to our officers. I was told stories of the public thanking officers at the stores and in public for their service, showing general appreciation for the job. That warmed me inside. The School Resource Deputy was kind enough to drop a bunch of handmade cards from the local elementary school kids. They were so adorable and loving and filled with kind words. In the long run I didn't have the space to store them and I knew that ultimately I would need to move on emotionally. So sometime early that summer I had a fire in my backyard by myself, in a new fire pit that was built for me while injured by my friend and partner, Detective Brian Podany. I chose to burn the cards from the kids in that new fire pit. Not in a negative way, but in the way you might burn a tattered American flag, with the honor and respect they deserved.

While I was doing that, I saw a squad drive by the front of the house. The driver saw the fire and came right to the backyard. It was Sergeant James Stuart. Sergeant Stuart, now Sheriff Stuart, and I were slowly becoming friends and he was on duty and wanted to see how I was doing. Nothing official, and that was appreciated. It became kind of ironic to me later. You see, while I was going through struggles with my Sheriff's Office administration, Sergeant Stuart and one other Deputy, Deputy Andrew Lindberg, became my main confidants, my "sanity support system" as I would call it. He also became Sheriff of Anoka County in 2011 and he did something that helped me on the path to finally healing. I'll share more on that later in the healing section of this book. And because during the next months I was getting so much flak from my Undersheriff for supposedly working up the other Deputies, for both Sergeant Stuart and Deputy Lindberg, I would periodically feed them different false details to see if they were leaking our conversations, and I'm proud to say no false information ever got back to me, meaning they were both trustworthy. I would say his visit is what solidified that we were true friends. The rest of it solidified that I could trust him. He stayed for a while as I burned cards and we chatted until it was time for him to go. I felt good about his visit that night.

CHAPTER 8
DETAILS, DETAILS, DETAILS

It was tough for me to get official details about the shooting since it was ruled a Homicide and I was part of the investigation. And before you jump to any conclusion reading that word, the ruling of "Homicide" occurs by a Medical Examiner whenever there is taking the life of human being by another human being. It is up to the criminal justice system to determine if it was lawful or not, but homicide does not automatically mean murder or manslaughter. That means that there were tons of interviews of neighbors, reports by any officer involved during or after the event, review of forensic evidence, ballistics, toxicology, and so on. On the night of the shooting there was also some kind of mix up in the order of details getting from my mouth to Sergeant Nolan to my Sheriff to the media. By the time it got to my administration it was communicated that the suspect shot me first and then I returned fire. This was then communicated by my agency to the media, which is probably why the media left me alone for the most part. Unfortunately, that added additional stress as they realized they had publicly released incorrect information. A reporter from KSTP Channel 5, a local Minneapolis/St. Paul TV News Station left me a few messages on my work voicemail but I wasn't interested in an interview and never called them back.

I gave an official statement nine days after the shooting. Most of the delay was because of being in the hospital and my initial transition to coming home. When I got home, I was being pulled in two different directions. As part of our union benefits, we get a Criminal Attorney to cover us during any serious investigation like this. My agency, both as my department and as the investigating agency, was expecting the interview as soon as possible while the Criminal Attorney assigned to my case was trying to block and delay the interview to allow for my healing and for me to be free of medications. I was a little confused and worried about what decisions to make regarding this and what to say and when to say it. If I decided to agree too early, it could negatively impact the criminal investigation if I said something wrong while medicated. But by holding out I would only anger my administration, which could later affect my career once this was all over with. I decided that by this time I had shared the story out loud many times anyway and I had nothing to hide. I knew it was a clean shooting. So I insisted my Attorney arrange it so we can finally get it done. The Detectives came to my house and I held off taking any pain meds that morning of the interview to avoid any problems. It was stressful reliving the shooting out loud in such an official capacity, mostly because it's not like I could stop and tell it as I wanted to. In most cases prior to this, I would tell it in chunks until I got stressed and would stop. But this was official and I couldn't do that so I cooperated fully. All in all, I felt happy the investigation could now carry on and official conclusions could be made faster. There were still some holes in understanding many of the aspects and details in the shooting for me, so getting the investigation over with would help me to get important details I've been aching to know.

Between talking to Sam, the conversation with the SWAT team that night in the hospital, talking to Deputies who had knowledge of the event, and begging a Crime Lab Deputy for a couple minor details, I eventually pieced together some missing parts. The suspect's name was Eric Nylen, a 29-year-old unmarried white male who owned the duplex he lived in and lived there alone while renting out the other half. He didn't have any kids or a wife. He didn't fit the norm of that particular neighborhood as far as police interactions. This was a troublesome area for Andover, which was filled with rental housing and had fairly frequent police calls to the neighborhood. However, there were no police calls for his address and he wasn't known for causing trouble. His uncle indicated in a statement that Mr. Nylen was previously in the Navy Reserves for about six years and he was skilled in firearms. He also had a Minnesota permit to carry a concealed firearm. He owned several long guns and hand guns, some placed in normal positions, and some placed more tactically in his house. The rifles and shotguns were propped up against corners in bedrooms. Two handgun cases, both with .45 caliber ammo but no guns in them, were in the open. On a shelf in the house was a cased .357 with ammo. On the kitchen table was an empty gun case with .45 caliber ammo and a left handed holster. Since that's where Nylen returned with a .45 caliber gun from, I presume that is the holster and/or case for the gun he used in the shooting. There was also a Colt .45 caliber semi-auto handgun on the same table. He also had a bullet reloader in the basement so he obviously did his own reloads, along with boxes of ammunition throughout the house.

He had no illicit or prescription drugs in his system. The initial toxicology blood screen for the Medical Examiner came back with a "positive indicator for benzodiazepine," which are frequently used to treat anxiety conditions, but on a "blood benzodiazepine quantitation" the result was "none detected." This meant it was either a false positive on the initial screen, and there was none in his system, or the amount was below the testing threshold indicating it likely wouldn't be a factor in causing the behavior. Mr. Nylen was in court earlier that day but for something against his previous employer and it sounds like it went positively for him. In all the interviews with friends and family, there was no reason to believe there were any personal stresses. We have no understanding why Mr. Nylen would respond to the doorbell with a gun in his hand or, more importantly, why he would ignore commands from Uniformed Deputies and point the gun at me.

When the shooting happened, I pulled my trigger twice but only heard a single "pop" from my own gun. Sam only reported hearing a total of three "pops," which made sense since Mr. Nylen's gun fired twice and mine apparently once. This detail complicated understanding the scene investigation a bit for Detectives and the Crime Lab Deputies because if I pulled my trigger twice, you would have thought there would have been four total shots. To complicate things on the scene further, one of my gun magazines held sixteen rounds, instead of the normal fifteen rounds, because of a compressed spring inside allowing sixteen rounds. So they would have expected that I carried 46 rounds (fifteen in each of the three magazines and one in my gun chamber). If I shot one round, they would expect to find forty-five rounds left in my gun and magazines. Instead they found forty-six rounds related to my gun. I explained it later and things made sense after that. Based on the ballistics and scene forensics, it was confirmed my gun only went off once and the single round struck the door before striking Mr. Nylen. I finally confirmed from Crime Lab that my gun had no obvious jams or stove pipe malfunctions. We can only guess that I pulled the trigger so fast that it didn't have a chance to fully recharge the trigger, thus firing only once.

The round that came from my gun struck the storm door in the metal area between the top half screen and the bottom half window. The bullet likely expanded somewhat from striking the metal and then entered Mr. Nylen in the chest to the right of the center line. The bullet punctured his right lung. Although he physically reacted when the bullet hit him, Nylen was able to track my flash light and do a "double tap" on me, which is a combat technique of shooting often taught in Law Enforcement in which you shoot twice in succession causing the two bullets to hit in a closer proximity in a successive action. The theory is that it causes trauma closer together in a successive action causing the body and the mind to feel the shock and stop the threat faster. I can tell you it worked almost perfectly because the combination shut me down pretty quickly. Alternatively, the round that hit him was a single shot and, although a lethal one, it didn't cause the same shock as a double tap as he was still able to battle back and even called 911 before succumbing to his gunshot wound.

A later review of the evidence and photos added interesting insight for me. I had just gotten a new pager holder the week before so I could clip it on the front of my duty belt. The second bullet struck the pager in its new location before entering my pelvic region. Instead of shattering the plastic, it dented the corner plastic, almost as if it melted it. It also dented the battery inside. Surprisingly there appeared to be rifling marks in the plastic which are distinct markings on a bullet left by the inside of the barrel. It's essentially the fingerprint of the gun. It was odd and I could only surmise that the heat generated by the firing of the bullet caused this. Even more enlightening was realizing that the bullet striking the pager first also altered its pathway. It very likely directing the damage away from my intestines, colon and bladder.

CHAPTER 9
MEDIA AND PERCEPTIONS

The media was pretty good to me in the situation. Like I had previously said, Channel 5 called and left me about five or six voicemails wanting to do an interview, but I wasn't interested. A man had lost his life and his family was most certainly hurting. I didn't feel there was any benefit to my own healing process to do an interview. There were no other negative media reports, and no negative spin on things. In Law Enforcement that is fairly rare. But then again, the media was provided with the wrong order of information by my department. Not intentionally, but it sure sent a whirlwind of back stepping and retribution in the background on the part of my administration as time went on. At least it sure felt that way. The misinformation happened sometime between me passing it along in the ambulance, and when it reached my Sheriff. The order of things was mixed up and it was put out in the media that Mr. Nylen had shot me twice and I had returned fire after being shot. And, of course, that's how they put it out to the public. But the reality is, I didn't give him a chance to shoot me, and instead I shot him first. Okay, who am I kidding here? I really believe it was a matter of who had the faster trigger pull that made the difference between his death and mine. And from that distance and him pointing his gun at my face from so close his would surely have been a lethal shot. Although the shooting was valid, the media vultures would likely have been circling had the correct order of things been released. After our office released the information the Sheriff and did a press conference at around noon the next day, investigators started to see and hear a differing story trickling in, from conversations I had with others who had gotten back to them, and the forensic investigation. It didn't match the whole story of me returning fire.

Based on the original story that Mr. Nylen had shot first and I had returned fire, my department decided to have our own agency do the investigation. What?! Investigating your own agency's officer involved in shooting is pretty uncommon, especially when it results in death. Actually, it's considered a conflict of interest and it's plain stupid. In Minnesota, it's usually the Bureau of Criminal Apprehension (BCA) that handles such conflict of interest investigations for Law Enforcement Agencies. That being said, it made me feel good to know the level of confidence they had in the validity of the shooting.

Ultimately, they spent the next day or so at the shooting scene at the duplex taking pictures, measurements, and collecting evidence. It became apparent to the Crime Lab Deputies, and the investigators, that the order of things they originally thought was true were not the facts. That resulted in Crime Lab Deputies questioning if they should even be involved with the investigation because of the conflict of interest. Our Crime Lab Deputies have an amazing sense of ethics and they knew they needed to be off the case and it turned over to another agency, if nothing else, to make sure there are no perceptions of impropriety. I was told that there was a heated situation with differences of opinion, which eventually led to a fairly loud argument in the middle of 140th Lane between a Crime Lab Deputy and his supervisor. The Deputy, understandably so, insisted that the case be given to another agency. But the supervisor he was arguing with and the upper administration didn't agree and Anoka County Sheriff's Office kept the case in-house. I want to reiterate though, our Crime Lab Deputies, now called the Crime Scene Unit, are some of the best Crime Scene Investigators in the state. And their desire to follow the right investigative path no matter what, only strengthens that opinion. And that opinion was confirmed once I had a chance to review the investigation file.

CHAPTER 10
MY RETURN TO LIGHT DUTY

I took a couple of months off work before I returned to light duty. I was dealing with both my administrative team at the Sheriff's Office and parallel communication with the Risk Management who handled the Worker's Compensation as well, I dealt mostly with a woman named Suzie. Anoka County was self-insured so they definitely stayed on top of "keeping in touch" during this process. Suzie would call me every week or two to check on my condition and pressure me about getting a timeline of when I would be returning to work. She was insensitive at best, and often used tones that made me feel like I should feel guilty for not being back to light duty yet. I absolutely HATED talking to her, but it was required since Work Comp was now paying part of my paycheck. Returning to work even to light duty must be approved by a doctor. My doctor didn't want to release me yet. He was concerned about any bump to my arm causing pain, and complications in healing properly.

Then, early in the summer before I returned, I heard that the Sheriff's Secretary, Joann Lien was retiring. She was a wonderful woman and the person I dealt with the most during my initial hiring process. She was having a cake social at the main Sheriff's Office and I ventured out. It was one of the rare outside trips I took at the time because I got tired so easily and if I was in a fender bender I would reinjure my arm pretty badly. But it was important to start getting out and interacting with people. While I was there, I happened to sit across the table from Suzie and Chris, from Risk Management. Suzie was asking light questions about my healing and Chris overheard something about me not being back on light duty yet. He turned around and said, "What, you aren't back on light duty yet?" I was shocked by the question and took a breath before answering. I explained that no I wasn't because my doctor didn't want me doing anything yet. They both commented that I should be back on light duty and kept telling me they couldn't believe I wasn't yet. They weren't belittling me or anything, but their comments were way out of line. I sat there trying to enjoy my cake and waiting for the right moment to congratulate Joann on her retirement. Instead, I was stuck dealing with these two bullies. I looked up at them and on the tip of my tongue were the words, "How about you take two 45 caliber rounds to your body and see how fast you get back to light duty?" Instead of saying these words out loud, I got up and left. Later that week I spoke to my Undersheriff, but he just blew it off. I told my doctor that they were pressuring me and I loved his answer. "Well, just hand her this note and let her know that's my decision, not hers." I sent her the note promptly, which kept me off work for longer.

Undersheriff King was my main point of contact while I was on early medical leave. We would talk every week or two to update my status. Up until Sheriff's Secretary Joann Lien's retirement cake social I hadn't been out of the house much, but I had periodic visitors. My partners would drop in to check on me and get me anything I needed. I was surprised that my administration didn't come by and see me as we were supposed to be family. Were they avoiding me? Or maybe they were busy. I tried to put it out of my mind as much as possible, writing it off as coincidence and reading too much into it. Either way, it was a part of my initial feelings of being abandoned by my administration.

I had been going to follow-up visits for Dr. Kraft every two to three weeks. Finally, in mid-July, Dr. Kraft said my healing was going well and if I thought I was ready maybe I could start out with a part-time light duty day. He made me promise not to try to be a cop, not to lift anything, and to take it easy. It was more about slowly building my stamina back up. The truth is, I was ready to get out of the house and be productive again. I returned to work on July 17, 2003, two months after the shooting. I only worked four hours a day but it felt good to be back at the Patrol Station and to be around my brothers and sisters of the badge. Mostly I did light paperwork. I was in charge of downloading pictures from digital cameras, taking a few phone calls, filing papers, and so on. It was exhausting at first but my doctor told me that was normal. He said regenerating bone was pretty taxing on the body and that was one of the harder bones in the body. Nevertheless, I enjoyed the time out of the house. By that time I was able to manage the pain with a milder painkiller. I stayed on my normal rotation of six days on and three days off. This was best for me because of my rotating parenting schedule with my son, since his mom and I were no longer together.

By the end of August, I started working six hours of light duty a day, and by the end of October I was cleared for eight hours a day, but no street duty yet. My arm seemed to be healing well. It was functioning for more normal use, with some weakness and, of course, numbness from the nerve damage. I had been working on a lot of random jobs and tasks. I even helped to clean out and organize the patrol evidence area. I liked having something to do each day as it made the days go by quicker. One of my favorite projects was working with Sergeant James Stuart on developing portions of his Active Shooter Training in response to the Columbine High School and other school shootings in recent years. It was fun helping him develop the materials and working the active portions of the training. Plus, it was a good test of how I would respond in a simulated shooting situation. All fared well with no physical or emotional issues popping up during the research and the active part of the training. That felt great since I had also been to the gun range a couple of times and didn't react to any of the gun fire.

I started to think about my own mortality, the shooting, and the idea that I had taken someone's life. I was comfortable with WHY I took his life, but it was always in the back of my head that it meant Mr. Nylen's family would never be able to see or hug him again. Although I have no doubts about the validity of having to shoot him, it wasn't their fault that this had happened. I didn't share those feelings with my administration or many people, as it was a pretty private thought process and I thought they may take it wrong. In September 2003, Calibre Press was hosting Lt. Colonel

Dave Grossman at a prison an hour south in Red Wing, which was my hometown. The training was an all-day event called "Bulletproof Mind: Mental Preparation for Combat." I asked for permission to attend, and my Patrol Lieutenant asked why I thought I needed to go. I said I felt it was important to get a perspective on the shooting and the death, and it would be good for me, and possibly Sam too. He didn't seem keen on the idea, but I made it clear I was going anyway, whether on my own by taking a day off, or with them sending me. They agreed and both Sam and I attended. I'm not sure what Sam did or didn't get out of it, but I felt an increased confidence that what I did was normal. I felt a strange disconnect with my administration over the shooting, so I needed this. I even got to personally meet Lt. Col. Grossman. He knew of me being involved in a shooting and gave me some great input and positive reinforcement. I was already sensing that the Sheriff had a different feeling about it, so I needed some validation and Grossman solidified it for me.

I also attended the Calibre Press Street Survival training in Milwaukee in January 2004 and received continued validation on the tactical concepts of the shooting. I hadn't heard the results of my department's administrative Review and I wasn't thrilled how they were avoiding supporting me, so I continued to search out support elsewhere. The administration seemed intent on withholding information and keeping me at a distance. They seemed more concerned about their own defense rather than supporting one of their officers. I struggled with that and couldn't figure out what they felt they needed to be on the defensive about. In my networking with officers outside my agency, I mentioned that I was okay, but trying to get a grasp on the death part. I mean, I've experienced quite a bit of death in my own life, and I had been to many death scenes on duty, but that didn't mean I had a full grasp on death itself. I can't remember by whom, but it was suggested that I attend an autopsy and get some closure on the part about death that I didn't understand. I approached Lt. Tom Wells about it, but he said he didn't think that was necessary. I was disappointed and irritated, but I was trying not to ruffle anyone's feathers in the hopes I would be able to return to full duty. Overall, Lt. Wells was a good guy, but perhaps ignorant when it came to understanding the mind. I do believe it would have helped.

CHAPTER 11
THE GRAND JURY

Anytime a person is killed at the hands of another, in most states it is considered a "Homicide," regardless of the legality of the death. This is also true in Minnesota. It was strange to see the paperwork go from "Attempted Murder/Officer Involved Shooting" with me being the "victim" to "Homicide" with Eric Nylen being the victim and me now being the "potential defendant." I understood it all as being an important part of the legal process, but scary nonetheless. On June 12, 2003, a month after the shooting, I received an "invite" to appear and testify in front of the Grand Jury. I had been in court to testify many times, but never in front of a Grand Jury. I knew the ramifications, too. It was a room of twelve to twenty-six citizens who were deciding on a variety of cases during their tenure, which included whether or not to indict me for the death of Nylen. Not testifying meant they would review the physical evidence and the statements of others, including my statement. For the most part, the Prosecuting Attorney would control and decide what is and is not included in grand jury, but often with Officer Involved Shootings they try to present as much of the available information to the Grand Jury to allow them to make their decision. I was allowed to have my attorney present in the room, but by rule he was not allowed to participate, object, and so on; only advise at certain times. If the Grand Jury decided to return a Bill of Indictment, then the County Attorney's Office would end up charging me for whatever level of murder or manslaughter they saw fit. Alternatively, if they chose not to indict me by returning a No Bill of Indictment, known as a "No Bill," then it would be up to the County Attorney's Office to decide from there, but in most cases they would not pursue any charges in the matter.

I chose to accept the invitation to testify at the Grand Jury hearing. I had been honest and had nothing to hide and didn't have any concerns over the validity of the shooting. My attorney didn't seem too concerned either and he was a pretty highly strung guy. The Grand Jury date that I testified on was on June 30, 2003. Upon arrival my Attorney was talking to me and discussing the day. But, to be honest, I have no idea what he was saying. I felt so nervous. The joke among Law Enforcement is that you are in the room with twenty-six potato farmers deciding your fate. It was one of the scarier moments of in my life.

The Prosecuting Attorney assigned to my case was Sean C. Gibbs, Assistant Anoka County Attorney (ACA). I didn't know Sean well, but I knew of him. We had run into each other here or there but that's about it. I didn't really trust him at that point because I was in such a vulnerable position. Police Officers aren't generally used to feeling vulnerable. And since this involved the potential for me being charged with manslaughter or murder, I had good reason to be nervous. I had a friend of mine that worked in the County Attorney's Office that shared a story with me about my case. This friend had overheard what was described as an argument between

ACA Gibbs and another Assistant Anoka County Attorney who I knew. This was all prior to the Grand Jury proceedings but I would hear about it afterwards. Although I was told it was an "argument," I envision it more as a heated debate at most based on how it was described, with no yelling or raised voices. Apparently, the other ACA asked about the case and mentioned, in a questioning fashion, that they thought I "was good, right?" I'm told that ACA Gibbs responded with "Well, Dustin did shoot him first..." with a concerning tone, which lead to the alleged heated discussion. That's pretty scary knowing that my shooting, which I was more than confident was justified, was up for so much debate prior to the Grand Jury proceedings. As a professional in the criminal justice field, I understand though. His job is to find the truth, whatever it may be. But his opinion on the case was a very important one and would guide the Grand Jury process. This is why I appreciated that hallway debate and any impact it may have had on ACA Gibbs thought process about the shooting. Too often there is a classic narrow-minded thought that police should only shoot after being shot or shot at. If I had waited for that I wouldn't be writing this story though, because I would likely be dead. ACA Gibbs was known to be a true professional so I was banking on that...nervously of course. And he proved to be just that. And I'm sure that is why he is now the Honorable Judge Sean C. Gibbs.

ACA Gibbs came out of the Grand Jury room to get me. My heart dropped. I was happy we were getting it over with but I couldn't help but feel nervous. As I walked into the room, there were a lot of Grand Jurors. I don't know exactly how many, but I would say twenty plus. As I walked into that room, each and every set of eyes looked at me. Some appeared to show pity, others curiosity, others still were blank. I feel I've always been a kind of master at reading people, but not that day, and especially not that many faces. I didn't take any painkillers that morning because I wanted to have a clear mind for the testimony. I stepped into the witness box and I was sworn in. ACA Gibbs led me through the shooting incident asking questions and getting clarification when needed. It started to get tough when we reached the details of the shooting. I became quite emotional as I explained the details of me getting shot and lying there thinking I was dying. So many memories, and especially emotions, flooded me all at once. They weren't new memories, but a new set of emotions had unleashed over the shooting details. I have a hard time talking when I get choked up and I hate crying in front of people, but that day I had no choice. The hardest point seemed to be discussing the vulnerability of me lying there only five to ten feet away from the same window I had been shot through and how I feared he was going to shoot me again. And discussing how I had to play dead, and hearing my partner's voice talk to me even though I now knew she thought she was talking to a dead person. But I got through it, having to take my time.

After my main testimony, some of the Grand Jurors asked if they could ask for some clarifications. I don't recall the questions they asked, but they were all reasonable and I answered every question with no concern about my future. ACA Gibbs thanked me and my Attorney and I left the room.

I was in shock. I was emotional, I had a headache from all the crying, and my arm was in agony by the end of it. My Attorney said it had gone great and now it was a 'hurry up and wait' process.

On July 3, 2003, only four days after the hearing, the Grand Jury came back with their decision. My attorney advised me that, after reviewing all of the evidence, my testimony and testimony of a couple of Use of Force Experts, they returned a "No Bill of Indictment" and furthered that the Anoka County Attorney's Office would not issue any charges on the matter. What a relief! Deep down I knew I was okay, but it was all so surreal.

CHAPTER 12
CONFLICTS AND STRESSES

I had a lot of friends in the department so information got back to me quicker than the administration would have liked. One sure example of that is when a good friend of mine, Sergeant Michael Longbehn, came up to me on light duty one day and he seemed upset. We often shared our stresses about work or home so I asked him what was up. He said, "It's about you." He then shared that he was at a Sergeant's meeting discussing my shooting when the Sheriff said to them, "I don't believe [Nylen] was going to shoot Dustin." WHAT??? I sat there and stared at Sergeant Longbehn in pure disbelief. He said, "I know!" I couldn't believe it. Where in God's name does he get off deciding if the guy was going to shoot me or not? He wasn't there. And he wasn't looking down the barrel of a 45 caliber Sig Sauer handgun. "That motherfucker" is all I could get out of my mouth. And I repeated it several times. I had thought it strange that he only visited the hospital once and never came to see me when I was laid up at home and never personally called me. But I was trying to accept that there must be legitimate reasons. I figured he must be busy or maybe there were official recommendations. Well, now I knew. I hoped to one day to find the right moment to get to talk to him about it. And in the meantime I tried to chug

95

forward regardless. My main focus was to get healthy and return to working the street. Sergeant Longbehn has since left Anoka County and now works for another Police Agency in Minnesota.

Parallel to a criminal investigation is an internal investigation with results that are given for two other processes: #1, a Shooting Review Board and #2, a Critical Incident Review. Normally, and by our policy, these were two separate processes. The Shooting Review Board had the task of reviewing the shooting and determining if the shooting was within policy. The Critical Incident Review was about reviewing the shooting to verify if there was any need to change training and/or policy. I was told about this by Captain Jenkins, my Patrol Division Captain, sometime during mid-summer. He told me they were going to combine the Shooting Review Board and the Critical Incident Review. At first I had no concerns about that. But the more I thought about it, the more I realized it was probably a bad idea. It was another standardized process to make reviews of shootings as impartial as possible that was now altered and the line blurred just as with investigating it ourselves. The truth is, the Sheriff had a reputation of headhunting our officers if they were acting at all contrary to his beliefs or the direction in which he wanted to go. At least that's how it felt to many of us. I could not trust my own Sheriff so I struggled trusting anything that came out of his administration. So this only added to my fears and concerns.

That being said, even he wouldn't be able to find a policy violation in this one, at least nothing worthy of providing me any realistic punishment. I say that because, just like laws, you can try to twist the truth and the laws or policies to try to fit and justify something. But again, I wasn't concerned. I had asked Captain Jenkins a couple of times how long it would take to complete the administrative Review and when it would be announced but he had said he wasn't sure. So summer passed into fall, and there were still no answers. I can't explain why, but it was grinding away at me that they weren't coming up with an official answer, and, more importantly, a public announcement to my partners and even the public that I was officially cleared of any violation. I had already been cleared by the Grand Jury, but for some reason I felt like it was vital that I hear it officially and that if be it be announced officially. I started to ask Captain Jenkins weekly and he would just say, "Don't worry about it, you've got nothing to worry about." Or statements like, "You'll be just fine, don't worry about it." But it bothered me quite a bit. It was getting harder and harder to let it go like I used to. I would eventually learn that my feeling was normal after traumatic events, needing validation and support from the administration. There are several suggested guidelines about dealing with and responding to traumatic and post shooting situations, the most notable from the International Association of Chiefs of Police (IACP). Of note in the Officer Involved Shooting Guidelines published by the IACP is Section 5.8 which says:

> *Unnecessarily lengthy investigations cause undue distress to officers. Agencies should make every effort to expedite the completion of administrative and criminal investigations...While investigations are pending, supervisors should maintain regular contact*

with officers and keep them apprised of any pertinent developments.[1]

Using guidelines such as this is especially important for agencies such as the Anoka County Sheriff's Office, which had very little experience with Officer Involved Shootings. I started to obsess over the idea that they weren't giving an official conclusion. I couldn't figure out why they wouldn't finish the Shooting Board and Critical Incident Review. I'd never heard of that happening before. I started to become increasingly apprehensive and concerned that he was pushing them to find some kind of violation.

On September 2, 2003 I received a memo from Captain Bob Aldrich from our administrative Division that advised that he was assigned by the Undersheriff to oversee Critical Incident Review #03-002. At first I laughed because I didn't know there was another Critical Incident that year besides mine! But then I read it a couple of times and it hit me. This was a notice that the "Administrative Investigation" essentially had just begun. I wondered why it had taken so long to start the review. I mean, it was now four months after the shooting, certainly much later than what was recommended. If they didn't want to follow or research the guidelines put forth by the IACP, maybe they could have considered calling a large agency, such as Minneapolis or St. Paul PD's to get advice

---

[1] International Association of Chiefs of Police Psychological Services Section, "Officer-Involved Shooting Guidelines," *International Association of Chiefs of Police, 2016,* www.iacp.org/portals/0/documents/pdfs/Psych-OfficerInvolvedShooting.pdf

in handling an Officer Involved Shooting. Unfortunately, in this case that isn't what happened. The memo went on to state the reasons and guidelines for an administrative Investigation, which all made sense. But then we got to the bottom and I read this:

> *"Please be advised that while the Administrative Investigation is active the information contained therein is classified as 'Confidential' and 'Private' pursuant to Sections 13.39 and 13.43 of the Minnesota Government Practices Act. You are asked to limit your discussions regarding this investigation to only those who are authorized access to this information by law. You are free to discuss the incident with your union representative(s) or legal counsel if you so choose."*

I thought to myself, *Are you shitting me???" They are delaying their job and I have to continue to keep it to myself?* They had already tried to prevent Sam and I from discussing it after it happened, and now this. Don't get me wrong, I completely understand that they need to have standards and limit discussions to keep the integrity of the review in place. But the integrity had been lost with the delays. And the stress of the actions of my administration, or more seemingly lack of actions, on top of dealing with the incident itself were really getting to me. I also have a strong theory that the requirements of me keeping it all in, not able to share with my partners, was starting to damage me inside. I could feel the pressure building inside. I was trying not to feel paranoid, but it was starting to feel peculiar to me. I have a great department so it was hard to imagine that our administration was blundering this so badly. It appeared they were delaying things on purpose, which, under the type of iron fist leadership that was in place at my department, could only mean it was at the direction of the man on top, my Sheriff. That being said, I kept talking myself out of such negative thoughts and tried to chug forward and return to healing. My long term goal was about returning to my squad and ultimately the Drug Task Force, not fighting the Sheriff.

I had been working through the winter on the various tasks assigned to me and trying to do them well and keep a positive attitude. However, the Sheriff's comment about him thinking Eric Nylen wasn't going to shoot me always stuck with me, and bothered me, almost on a daily basis. That meant my boss was questioning my word, my integrity, and my perception on the need to use deadly force. I continued to ask Captain Jenkins almost every week or two if they had wrapped up the Critical Incident Review and he always gave me answers such as, "Not yet, but it should be soon," or, "I don't know how long, but you know you're good." Finally, I told him in December, in response to such comments, "NO, not with this Department. We don't ever know we're good. We don't trust our administration, I certainly don't. I can't explain why, but all I can tell you is that it's overwhelmingly important that you guys finally clear me. I think it'll help me to heal emotionally and send a clear message. The delays make it seem like there's an issue or trying to find an issue." Captain Jenkins reassured me there was nothing to worry about. I was as professional as I could be when I was talking to him, but I was very direct during that time period. Enough was enough. I told him that I needed this wrapped up or I would ask the union to get involved. It had been seven months by now. I reiterated that it was eating me alive. In my later research I found out that my feelings were not uncommon. It felt like they were trying to keep me hidden, like I was the shameful stepchild they didn't want.

And then I finally hit my breaking point. One day in January of 2004, I was downloading some crime scene and accident photos from memory cards. We did this in an office and on a computer primarily used by our Crime Prevention Specialist. It was a weekend and she wasn't there so I was leaning back in the chair waiting for the images to transfer. I glanced over and on her desk beside me I saw a memo and noticed the word "Awards" dated January 22, 2004. It didn't say confidential and it was out in the open so I was nosy and I took a peek. Each year the Sheriff's Office gives out a variety of awards. Some are really earned, while others are fluff awards, and there are many in between. It read:

"The proposed awards agenda is as follows..."

And the second award down was my name. It said:

"Deputy Reichert will receive a Purple Heart as a result of being the <u>VICTIM</u> of a shooting."

Victim??? Victim??? What??? That set me on a blaze of different feelings. Okay, technically I was a victim. But when it comes to awards there are so many other ways to word it. Survivor of a violent shooting is one that comes to mind. By this time I was already feeling crappy about how the shooting was being handled, so I was trying to keep myself in check, telling myself I was overreacting. But it was getting tough. Right after that it read:

> "Officers Scott Nolan and J Casey (Anoka PD), J Urquhart and D Keasling (Coon Rapids PD) and J Omann (Blaine PD) to receive a Medal of Merit for their efforts rescuing Deputy Reichert."

Well, good, they got that one right. I was proud and honored that they were receiving awards for their hard work rescuing me. But wait a minute. Where was Deputy Samantha Cruze on that list? As I steamed for a while and looked again, I couldn't believe it. They had awards for attempts to resuscitate someone who hanged them self, for someone's head being held up out of water when their car flipped, for Detectives cases on homicides, and an internal theft. All of which I had no problem with. But a Deputy, two days on her own, standing by and covering her partner after he had been shot, risking her life even though she thought I was dead. If that didn't deserve an award then I'm not sure what did. I was so upset that I sat there for a while, steaming, as I recalled a past incident when another Deputy shot a suspect once when he pointed a gun, ironically hitting the gun with the single shot. That gun turned out to be a lighter-shaped like a gun and it was sent to the Minnesota Sheriff's Association for a Medal of Valor. And rightfully so. But we were in a real life actual gun battle and she didn't get recognized for her bravery and professionalism, and I got recognized for being a "victim." I didn't need the Medal of Valor, but I deserved to be recognized as more than a victim. I tried to remain calm but I think that was the last straw for me. It became clear that my department, specifically my

Sheriff, was ashamed of the shooting and wanted to make it go away as quietly as possible. I don't know his true feelings but that's how it felt to me.

By the time I got down the hall I had calmed down a bit. I wasn't sure how I was going to finish the shift without talking to anyone, because that was my only way to avoid exploding. And I was right. The Community Service Officer (CSO) for Andover came in while I was in the Report Room. We were friends and she could tell I was upset. She kept asking and I said I needed some time to settle down and I would tell her later. She pushed, and my gasket blew. By the time I was done spewing the steam of rants and curse words about the Sheriff saying the guy wasn't going to shoot me, how they seemed to be embarrassed by me, how they won't make an official decision about the shoot being good or not, and so on, I had a crowd of Deputies around me coming in from work and finishing their shift. I stopped spewing, my face red, and tears welled up in my eyes that I was fighting so they wouldn't show. Sergeant Plattner and Sergeant Orlando were in the Sergeants room and also came down. Once it was over they dispersed the group and Sergeant Plattner handled the roll call while Sergeant Orlando talked to me privately. I explained what had happened, which had led to the outburst. She did her best to calm me down, but I could tell she didn't truly understand. She tried to explain to me all the ways the Department was supporting me, but in reality, those were mostly individual acts by my partners and friends, not by the Department itself, and certainly not by my administration. I apologized because I didn't want it to come out that way and I shouldn't have handled it that way. I told her that I needed to head home for the day to further calm down and avoid talking to anyone else that day. She agreed and I went home

The next day I returned to work and did my best to work hard and, once again to keep moving forward. I was embarrassed about my outburst as I was better than that. But it happened and all I could do was make up for it. I avoided bitching and complaining publicly to repair the damage the outburst had already done. I finally had a meeting with the Sheriff. That's right, the man on top actually asked me to come in. I was nervous because of my outburst, but when he was a Captain we had a pretty good relationship. In his office I apologized about the outburst. He said I obviously I had some concerns and he told me to speak freely. I responded by asking if he truly meant it and he said, "Yes, but be respectful." I felt relieved to be able to speak freely to him. I shared with him my frustrations about the administrative review and how it looked like they were embarrassed by the shooting and they were appearing to try to sweep it under the rug. I told him it appeared they were embarrassed by the mis-reported information to the media, and they seemed to be backtracking, leaving me in the damaged trail of it all. He listened quietly, red-faced, which happened when he was angry, but he quietly listened nonetheless. And then I shared with him what I heard about him saying at the Sergeants meeting that he didn't think Mr. Nylen was going to shoot me. I asked him if he had said that and he responded, "I don't deny it." I reminded him that is exactly how I was trained both in Law Enforcement Skills Program, by the Ramsey County Sheriff's Department, and by the Anoka

County Sheriff's Office itself. And I said, "Actually, if I didn't pull the trigger you should probably be asking for my badge and gun because I obviously couldn't protect anyone." I felt that way then, and I still feel that way now. I also made it clear that, as I stared down that barrel of that 45 caliber gun from an extremely close distance, there was no doubt when a man points a gun at your chest and then moves it to between your eyes, he wants to take your life, or wants you to believe he's going to take your life. The difference, I told him, was who had the faster trigger pull, and there was probably only half a second difference. It was quiet in his office for about ten to twenty seconds. I assume he was taking in everything I had just said and probably mad about my bluntness. And as direct as I was, I was keeping my emotions under wrap after discussing such intimate details of the shooting. The Sheriff tried to tiptoe around the subject and said he would get the Critical Incident Review Committee going and take my concerns into consideration. I don't know what I expected, but knew that was probably the best I would get from him.

My opportunity to be open with him was a double-edged sword. It released quite a bit of built up pressure brewing inside me, which was desperately needed, but it also likely released another level of suspicion and defensiveness by the Sheriff. This meant I would likely pay the price soon enough. It was obvious I made him angry and I knew what that probably meant.

I returned for a visit with my Orthopedic Surgeon, Dr. Kraft, on February 19, 2004 and he told me I could return to full duty on February 27, 2004. I was struggling with some weakness, numbness, and pain, but I felt like I would be okay going back to duty and I was somewhat vague with the Dr. about my ongoing symptoms. After all, I was a cop and I needed to get back to it.

On February 27, 2004, I received a memo from the Undersheriff stating:

> *"We are in receipt of the medical workability report from your physician, which effective February 27, 2004, removes previously imposed physical restrictions, however, at this time, you have not been cleared for full duty.*

> *Effective Saturday, February 28, 2004, your new duty assignment will be in the Administrative Division. Therefore, you are not scheduled to work this Saturday, February 28 or Sunday February 29. Please report to me at my office, on Monday March 1, 2004 at 8:30 a.m. Your new work schedule will be Monday through Friday, 8:00 a.m. to 4:30 p.m. Your duties and responsibilities will be clarified at that time."*

I received the memo on Friday of that week. My administration was notorious for providing memos of questionable subject on Fridays to allow for the situation to cool off for the weekend. But they never seem to recognize the anxiety it creates for the Deputy receiving it. I had all weekend to think about the potential implications of the memo and how my response, whatever it would be, would be interpreted by the administration. If my doctor released me, why had my Sheriff's administration not cleared me for duty? Why, of all positions to be assigned, would they put me in an administrative position? Was it because the administrative Review wasn't complete yet or was there another motive? Their actions since the shooting hadn't been "normal" so I wasn't sure what to think anymore. On top of the personal stress that the memo caused, they had changed my hours and days off, which created logistic problems with the split parenting schedule I had with the mother of my 6-year-old child. Most people might think that I could easily work things out with my ex, but she wasn't easy to work with in these situations and it went smoother for us when we didn't alter the parenting schedule. Undersheriff King's memo certainly ruined my weekend! I was so upset and couldn't believe that a clean shoot, and administration screw ups, could lead to a Deputy being treated like this.

I'm guessing that my previous conversation with the Sheriff and my outburst prior to that had put a target on my back. Only one day after that doctor visit and turning in my medical clearance form, I was advised that I needed to complete a psychological evaluation, specifically a fitness-for-duty evaluation. Both the Undersheriff and our Human Resources Manager assured me that this was "standard" in the case of a shooting. I asked if it was because of my outburst and was reassured by both of them that it had nothing to do with my outburst and only because I was involved in a shooting, especially since I had been shot and another person had died. I didn't second guess it too much since that made sense and it was a common practice among police agencies throughout the country. I told them I would have to consult with my union first but anticipated no issues.

Then, in March 2004, I was given a memo signed by the Undersheriff that stated I was "ordered" to report to a specific psychologist's office. I tensed up immediately! "ORDERED?!?!?!?" All I could think was, *Who the fuck do these guys think they are?* I was so tired of this bully attitude, these secret back room meetings, and the failure to finish the Critical Incident Review. Why didn't they just tell me they had arranged for my fitness-for-duty evaluation and give me the time and place? Why did they have to put it in the form of an order? What the hell did I do wrong? It was pretty apparent that something was wrong. Sure, it could have been a misused word, but I doubted it. The wording used in the letter didn't sound like the Undersheriff – it was more likely written by our Human Resource Manager, who I didn't trust at all. I kept calm and contacted my union to advise them. By this time, I got our Union Attorney Marylee Abrahams involved who said to go ahead and agree to the evaluation. She said we would meet or talk before to review what to expect. It was originally scheduled on March 8, 2004 but it changed to March 9, 2004. I don't remember if it was a change on my behalf or on the behalf of the department. What I can tell you is that it likely changed the course of my career since it changed who the evaluating doctor would be.

I was now assigned to Dr. Michael Campion who was a psychologist based out of Springfield, Illinois. I was told he was previously a Minneapolis Police Officer, so I felt slightly more at ease knowing that. However, this transpired to not be true. He did work for Minneapolis Police at one point, but, from what I can tell, only in a psychological capacity. One of his listed specialties was providing fire and law enforcement pre-employment and fitness-for-duty assessments for various municipalities throughout the upper Midwest. Later, in an online search, I discovered that he is a very conservative psychologist who had been let go by at least two agencies, which were later litigated with results on both sides. The search also shows that he had been sued or part of litigation by other officers who were terminated by their agencies after he provided fitness-for-duty evaluation. I felt mixed feelings. I reviewed the cases based on available information and it appeared the similarity to my case was him potentially missing a diagnoses of PTSD and claiming that personality disorders were the underlying cause of the reasons for referral. At least two of the cases involved a differing of opinions among psychologists who did follow-up evaluations and had disagreed with his diagnosis.

In the meantime, it was time to return to work, now at the main office. I was married by then and my wife, my mother, and my union attorney all convinced me to approach the situation calmly and as positively as possible. This wasn't easy, but that's the approach I took. I arrived that Monday morning in the Undersheriff's office. We spoke lightly and I kept any grumbling to myself. I did let him know this was going to create some serious problems in my parenting schedule but I was determined to approach it with a positive mind. Well...at least until he told me my initial assignment. I was told I would work in the gun permit window accepting applications and answering questions. My stomach dropped. There wasn't even an official position for this, at least at the time, and it was normally done by the records tech who was working the front desk, and the permits were processed by retired Officers and retired Deputies now working part time. I was anticipating at least being brought back to a position where I could use my talents rather than a clerical position.

As I sat at that desk for the first time, I couldn't believe it. I knew the records techs and enjoyed interacting with them, but it felt like I was being punished. I was a kickass, fun loving street and drug cop. I was a warrior who had undergone the battle of his life, nearly losing his own life and taking another's life, and here I was sitting in this fishbowl looking window. I was steaming…I was embarrassed…I was hurt…and I felt defeated. My agency was turning on me. The same agency I nearly gave my life for. Even if they weren't purposely trying to be that way, perception is reality and the perception was that they were. Regardless, I was a big boy and I had to move forward and stay positive. I knew a lot of people at the main office and had a lot of friends, so I had many visitors. Plus, Sergeant Stuart's office was nearby so I visited him frequently. He became my confidant and the person I privately vented to in order to keep my sanity. He and I would spend many lunchtimes together or else I would spend them with another Deputy working in the courts, Deputy Andrew Lindberg, who I got to know well.

I worked my way into the gun permit room while one of the guys was on vacation. I was so happy to be out of the fish bowl of the front windows and do something to keep myself busy. The gun permits were pretty easy, but I found it interesting to learn. I then was asked to research other agencies policies on internships and write a recommended internship. Again, I was happy to do this and I took it seriously. It kept me busy and I was learning new things. My partners back at Patrol and even in the Main Office were asking me a lot of questions, but I tried to keep things quiet and positive, relying on my two new confidants. I was confronted more than once by the Undersheriff about rumors of me having more "outbursts" like I had Patrol and getting the other Deputies riled up. I tried to reassure him that wasn't true but that fell on deaf ears. I had no idea where the rumors were coming from since I was almost totally isolated from my peers. As I mentioned earlier, I did have two confidants in the department, Sergeant James Stuart and Deputy Andrew Lindberg. I had already passed on small pieces of false information to both of them to see if they could be trusted, but that information never got out. I later learned that not being able to discuss what was happening to me is detrimental to working through PTSD, so thankfully I had the limited discussions with those two Deputies. If I had not had those conversations I dread to think the damage it would have done inside me. Sharing with non-Law Enforcement doesn't have the same effect. The truth is, I couldn't have given a rat's ass about what stress the rumors caused the administration. But the pressure and decisions they made because of what they thought I was doing based on the rumors were causing me tons of stress, so maybe I should have re-evaluated my concern. But since I wasn't the one doing it, I'm not sure I could have done anything to stop it.

CHAPTER 13
FITNESS-FOR-DUTY EVALUATION

March 9, 2004 came and it was time for the psychological evaluation. It had been ten months since the shooting. I had a previous meeting with my attorney, Marylee, and she told me to relax and be friendly. She said to answer the questions as completely as possible, but to remember that the evaluator is not my friend. "No problem, open and friendly, but protected, right?" She simply replied, "Yes." I was told that the fitness-for-duty evaluation would be done by Dr. Campion in Arden Hills and that's the release forms I signed for. I noticed that the memo ordering me to report for a psychological test was to the office of Dr. Gary Liaboe, then of Aden Woods Psychological Services. I was already at the location when I realized it was Dr. Campion I was supposed to see, but I knew he was out of Illinois so I figured it was a shared space. The appointment was at 8:45 a.m. and I didn't get much sleep the night before, but I was plenty energetic and awake. Maybe that was my fight or flight mechanism inside me. Regardless, I was apprehensive and a little nervous, but knew I needed to do this.

I waited in the waiting room and then Dr. Liaboe came out and introduced himself and invited me into his main office area. As I walked into his office I assessed the room, observed the details, a behavior ingrained into me during my years as a Patrol Deputy and a Detective in the Drug Task Force. I glanced at the certificates on the wall, which all were for Dr. Liaboe and none for Dr. Campion. As he invited me to sit down, my protective wall started to grow quickly. From what I understood, I was supposed to be meeting Dr. Campion, not this guy, or so I thought. I sat quietly for a moment and then figured I would move forward so I couldn't be accused of being uncooperative. I had been through other pre-employment evaluations when applying for police agencies, which were pretty much the same thing as a fitness-for-duty evaluation, and had passed. The lay term in the Law Enforcement world is "psychological evaluation" or "psych eval" for both. Plus, I figured we now automatically had a reason to challenge and appeal the results if they didn't go my way. Intellectually I knew I'd be okay, but emotionally I was still anxious and nervous. As we got into it, he asked me if I remembered his name. At that point, I didn't fully and said "umm…Leebo, Loubo, Linboe, something like that. I apologize for not remembering." He told me he was impressed, as most people don't get it right. I said, "Don't give me too much credit, I just remembered seeing it on your certificate behind me."

We discussed life details from where I was born, work history, current residence, medical history, and family makeup. He then had me do some activities that were test-like. He gave me a list of things to remember and then recall the items five, ten, fifteen, and even twenty minutes later. Here are some other test examples:

- *Add 3 + 3*

- *Subtract 2 from 9*
- *Multiply 5 x 5*
- *Add 14 + 17*
- *Subtract 8 from 56*
- *Multiply 5 x 21*
- *Subtract 7 from 100 repeatedly to six places*

Math comes easy to me so those were pretty easy. And since I enjoy challenge games, I immersed myself in the challenge to keep my mind off the pressure of the situation. Other tests included:

- *Spell the word "W-o-r-l-d" backwards*
- *Explain what "Don't count your chickens before they hatch" means.*
  - *My answer: "Don't rush in and just rely on the assumed outcome until you know what it is going to be."*
- *Explain what "Don't cry over spilled milk" means.*
  - *My answer: "There are bigger issues in life than what some people are dealing with, so sometimes it's not worth being upset."*
- *Explain how a bucket and a mug are similar and different.*
  - *My answer: [same] "Designed to hold liquid, both are cylinder and have one opening". [different] "One is larger and both have handles, but they are located in different places."*
- *Tell what I would do if I found a sealed and addressed envelope with a stamp on it.*

> ○ *My answer: "I would mail it."*
> * *Tell what I would do if I was the first person to discover a fire in a theater.*
>> ○ *My answer, "I would call 911."*

I found it interesting but very odd, so I still felt a little nervous. I had the voice of my union attorney running through my head to keep calm and be cooperative. So I kept as grounded as I could. He mentioned to me that he was surprised because people don't normally do that well with all of the tests. I told him I liked a good challenge, but right after saying it, I realized he probably didn't mean that in a good way. I certainly didn't want to stand out, so my wall went up even further. We also spent part of the day doing the normal psychological tests done in Law Enforcement prescreening, including the (Minnesota Multiphasic Personality Inventory (MMPI) and other similar tests. Basically, they ask a variety of reasonable and strange questions, many of them repeated with different wording. Strangely, I find those that are worded differently are worded differently enough to warrant a different answer. I'm not a "black and white" person, as there's too much grey in the world for straight yes or no answers, so I tend to read all the possibilities in answering. But I answered them to the best of my ability.

I continued my openness until we reached a point during an interview when I hit my wall. He asked about visits I've made to see the doctor over the last couple of years. When I mentioned my multiple recent visits from "the shooting" Dr. Liaboe paused, looked up at me and said, "Wait, you were in a shooting?" I froze. Imagine how in the movies they change the depth of field and focus as it zooms out. That's how it felt to me. My hands started sweating and my heart rate felt like it tripled. I'm sure my rate of breath suddenly increased. I responded, "Um, you know I've been in a shooting right?" He said no, he wasn't aware. I said, "That's the whole reason I'm here!" That was enough to raise my defense shield all the way up. Any answers I gave after that were much shorter and much more guarded.

After the test day was done I headed home feeling upset and betrayed. I didn't sleep much that night either, for the second night in a row. How could my agency do this to me? At that moment I knew something was going on behind the scenes with my Sheriff that I was unaware of. I no longer felt my observations and concerns were unreasonable. I realized that I was no longer being unreasonably paranoid. If they weren't putting me through the psychological evaluation because of the shooting, then why? I could only conclude it was because of my outburst and their listening to the rumors. The next day I returned to work and I went to see the Undersheriff. I let both he and the Human Resource Manger know my concerns about never meeting Dr. Campion and the fact that Dr. Liaboe never even knew I was involved in a shooting. They both blew it off and said everything was okay. My HR manager said, "Don't worry about it; they know what they're doing." Of course, they didn't have their careers on the line, so what did they care? And they weren't the ones being railroaded.

I called my attorney and let her know everything. She wasn't happy about Dr. Campion not being involved and the fact that Dr. Liaboe didn't know I had been in a shooting prior to the test day. She said she would look into it. My attorney told me it was a waiting game and hopefully we would have some answers soon, maybe within two to four weeks. So you can imagine my surprise as March turned into April, which turned into May, and there was still no answer on the results of the fitness-for-duty evaluation. I was pretty upset and frustrated. Another phase that should have taken no longer than thirty to sixty days was now excessively delayed again. During this time I finished the recommendations for the policy on internships. I tried to stay busy. Sergeant Stuart borrowed me for a while to work on an active shooter training program to address shootings such as the Columbine High School shooting incident. That task took me away from some of the pressures and gave me something worthwhile and satisfying to do.

On April 28, 2004, the Anoka County Sheriff's Office Annual Awards Ceremony finally came. It was a bittersweet situation. When they read a brief summary of my shooting, I got pretty emotional standing there. I was proud to see Sergeant Nolan from Anoka and Sergeant Urquhart both receive Medals of Merit for their actions in coming to my rescue. I was also upset that even after my pleas, Sam didn't receive anything. Later, Undersheriff King said to me, "You looked a little emotional, how come?" I don't even think I answered him because the question was so stupid to me. How could I not be emotional listening to them describe the event, and reliving moments of it? At least I was authorized to wear my uniform for the awards ceremony. It felt great to be back in my uniform, even if it was only for show. The next day I was invited to the Anoka Police Department Awards

Ceremony. Chief Wilberg said he hoped I would be there to present Sergeant Nolan with his award. When I mentioned that to the Undersheriff, he seemed annoyed that they didn't ask through our department. Then he denied my request to wear my Class A Dress Uniform and said, "You can wear a suit, you don't need your uniform." I couldn't believe it. I was still an officer, but that I was not allowed to wear my uniform when presenting such a prestigious award to someone who risked his life for mine, didn't make any sense to me. As annoying as his answer was, I wasn't surprised. The following night I proudly handed Sergeant Scott Nolan his Gallantry Star Award for his bravery on the night of my shooting.

By May, a year after the shooting, my attorney and I were pushing for some answers. I had been cleared medically in February, had complied completely with my duties, did the fitness-for-duty evaluation, had kept to myself, and still wasn't getting any cooperation or answers on the status of my employment. Finally, by May 2004 I was called into Sheriff Andersohn's office. This was both nerve wracking and exciting at the same time since this had to be the fitness-for-duty evaluation results. Exciting because they were finally here and I couldn't imagine I had "failed it." And nerve wracking because it felt strange that the Sheriff was the one calling me in. Maybe, just maybe, he was going to clear me and apologize for what had been going on and what they had been putting me through. I really wanted to return to my normal Duties. When I got there, our Human Resources Manager was in there too. When both of them are present, that usually meant the news wasn't going to be good. Any time she was involved, it meant someone was in trouble and in this case it was me. I paused for a minute, took a deep breath, and then gained composure as I entered the office, sitting across from the Sheriff at his desk.

He informed me that they had called Dr. Campion and got the fitness-for-duty evaluation results over the phone. The Sheriff said, to his own surprise, that I had "failed the psych eval," citing that Dr. Campion stated that I was "narcissistic" and "histrionic" and should never have been in law enforcement. He said that Dr. Campion explained these traits come on during late teens and early adulthood and are essentially untreatable. As you can imagine I sat there in complete shock. I was speechless.

After a short pause to process what I had been told, I asked what that meant for my employment and what we do from here. He said, "Well, that's why she's here. Dustin, it's a total shock to me too, so we have to figure things out together." I too was shocked. So many emotions overwhelmed me that tears welled up in my eyes. When I cry, my throat closes and I can't talk so I didn't say much after that. I was so stunned that I didn't know what else to say. As I left the office, I asked the Sheriff to please find a place for me in the Department. I don't usually resort to begging, but I loved this job and I was good at it.

As instructed, I followed our Human Resources Manager to her office. My career felt like it was in her hands. I wasn't sure that was a good thing. I wasn't even close to being a fan of hers. Most of the department felt the same way. Her title said "Human Resources Manager" but I think it should go back to the title of the old days of "Personnel Manager," which more accurately indicates her behavior of only seeming to represent the agency. I had never seen her acting positively or supportive towards low level staff. As we sat there, I wasn't sure what to say. I asked her if this meant I can't be a cop anymore, or just not on the street or what. Her response was, "Well, Dr. Campion said you should never have been a cop, so I don't know." I asked if I couldn't be a Deputy anymore, did I qualify for retirement? And would it be the 60 percent or the non-duty early retirement rate of 30 percent? She responded with, "I don't know, since he said Narcissism and Histrionics are usually present late teens or early adulthood, so it was before you were with Anoka County." She was essentially telling me that, not only might I no longer have a job, but that I might not be eligible for full retirement and my whole livelihood was at risk. What kind of "human resources" manager spews this information without getting factual information? I don't even remember leaving the office. I was numb from the news I had gotten from the Sheriff, and I was stunned with the impersonal attitude and lack of answers from my HR Manager. Before I left I told her, "Well, I always thought I might want to go see a therapist just in case, but I was hoping it'd be on my terms." She said she would help me find someone. She, of course, ruined her helpful behavior when I asked for it to be someone who specializes in police and she responded with, "Oh, that doesn't matter. You guys always think everyone needs to specialize in police for everything." In my head I was screaming, "Worst Human Resources Manager ever!" I snuck out of the office without many people seeing me and headed home.

On the way home my emotions were all over the place. I was both anxious and angry. I was worried about my future. What would I do if I couldn't be a cop? I had spent six years prepping for this job and another four plus years working hard at it. How was I going to tell my family? How was I going to support my family? My mind was racing. I was so keyed up by the time I got home, I felt like I would explode. I notified my attorney. I was still in an agitated state of mind, but needed to talk to someone. When I calmed down many questions popped in my mind, a few of which were:

1. Where's the written report? Since this effects someone's career, shouldn't it have been delivered as a written report?
2. Why did I get evaluated by Dr. Liaboe, but Dr. Campion is giving the report?
3. Why is Campion giving a psychological evaluation on someone he's never met or spoken to?
4. What about the pre-employment psychological test I "passed" when I joined the Anoka County Sheriff's Office?
5. What about the pre-employment psychological test I "passed" when I was licensed part-time with the Ramsey County Sheriff's Department?
6. What about the psychological tests I took before the Law Enforcement Skills Program that I "passed" in college?
7. Who uses the term "failed" when discussing a psychological test when in official capacity? People don't actually "fail" psychological evaluations. I can't be sure that was a term that came down from

Dr. Campion, but he's the one who chose to give the results to my administration over the phone.
8. Why was my department depending so much on Dr. Campion's evaluation and ignoring the two they had prior?

It didn't take my attorney and I long to kick into fight mode and the first step usually starts with a union grievance. As it turned out, my union attorney went to the same church as Dr. Liaboe. She said she understood that he was a family therapist. She questioned why he had conducted the evaluation and how he was qualified and said she would dig into it. It was difficult to file a grievance until we had a chance to read the actual written report by Dr. Campion. That official report didn't come for several more months. Since we didn't have Dr. Campion's written report, we filed a grievance without it. In our initial process in grieving the fitness-for-duty evaluation we focused on the lack of an official written report and the fact that Dr. Campion had never met or talked to me, yet was making a career-ending evaluation. As a result of that grievance, I received a memo from the Undersheriff ordering me (there goes that word again) to go to a follow-up appointment on June 14, 2004 with Dr. Campion. I found that ironic because I never had an initial appointment with him, so how can I do a "follow-up?" Meeting with him now didn't negate the fact that he gave an evaluation without ever having met or talked with me. This "follow-up" meeting was in response to our complaints that Dr. Campion had never met or talked to me. And my trust level was a bit low at that point. It felt like a cover-up by someone.

In the meantime, we were already developing our own strategy for taking on the Sheriff's administration. I was scheduled to take my own independent psychological evaluation for fitness-for-duty with Dr. Gordy Dodge, a psychologist who specializes in trauma and disaster. My union attorney sought out and was recommended to send me to Dr. Dodge who is well known for work with Police and Military and Post Traumatic Stress Disorder. The only way the Sheriff's Office would agree to a postponement with Dr. Campion is if I agreed to sign a release to share Dr. Dodge's evaluation with Dr. Campion. I found that strange since Dr. Campion had supposedly already completed his evaluation. We still hadn't gotten any official written report and he wanted Dr. Dodge's report? But on the advice of my attorney, I agreed to sign the release. I was kind of stuck between a rock and a hard place. If Dr. Campion got a copy of Dr. Dodge's report prior to completing his written evaluation, it could potentially alter his report. It seemed to me that they should be independent reports. However, if I refused to see Dr. Campion or give them a copy of Dr. Dodge's report, I would be punished for insubordination, including potentially being terminated.

In the meantime I continued to try to do my assigned work and keep a low profile. My union attorney told me to try to keep it to myself and keep things low key, not to give the Sheriff any ammo against me. So that's what I did, but that didn't go over well with my co-workers. My partners from Patrol, most of which were friends, and Detectives in the main office, several were also friends, had a lot of questions. And those who knew me all knew I wore my life on my sleeve, ready to share and not too worried about what people thought about my life. So when I suddenly stopped sharing what was going on, it raised a lot of red flags and my colleagues asked more and more questions. It left me feeling isolated, and not being able to share my frustrations with my friends started to eat me alive inside, leading to a strain on friendships. It felt like my department had gone from showing a lack of support to railroading me, and all while I was under the stress of trying to move on from the shooting. I was splitting at the seam and it became hard to sort out my emotions. I was on a worse emotional roller coaster than before my "blow up" at the Patrol Station. I felt angry, anxious, and worried all at the same time.

My fitness-for-duty evaluation results came in from Dr. Gordy Dodge, and I did a second interview with him on June 29 after he had all of the test results. He told me that his recommendation was to clear me for full duty but to continue seeing my therapist that I had begun seeing after the initial Dr. Campion verbal diagnosis as that would be best for optimum recovery. He said he felt I was suffering from Post-Traumatic Stress Disorder (PTSD), more specifically "Agency Induced PTSD." He said he may not word it that way in the official report though, otherwise my agency might push back too hard. I told him if it was the truth to write it that way. I received the written report less than a month later on July 22, 2004. It didn't include the phrase "Agency Induced PTSD," but it did officially list me as having PTSD. It also included a blurb stating, "What also is important to keep in mind is that after an officer involved shooting, if the officer perceives that he does not have administrative support and approval for his or her actions, some mistrust, resentment, and irritability often occurs for a while, these ironically not always presenting the officer in the most favorable light."

In the midst of all of this, I started to read and get an understanding of what Narcissism, Histrionic, and Post Traumatic Stress were. The Mayo Clinic, which is headquartered in Minnesota, says this about PTSD on their website:

Post-traumatic stress disorder (PTSD) is a mental health condition that's triggered by a terrifying event — either experiencing it or witnessing it. Symptoms may include flashbacks, nightmares and severe anxiety, as well as uncontrollable thoughts about the event.

Many people who go through traumatic events have difficulty adjusting and coping for a while, but they don't have PTSD — with time and good self-care, they usually get better. But if the symptoms get worse or last for months or even years and interfere with your functioning, you may have PTSD.[2]

A variety of other sources provided similar definitions. Everything I read about PTSD said it is treatable. The symptoms listed were all consistent with what I was going through. Dr. Dodge stated in his report that my behaviors

[2] Mayo Clinic, "Diseases and Conditions: Post-traumatic stress disorder," *Mayo Clinic*, www.mayoclinic.org/diseases-conditions/post-traumatic-stress-disorder/basics/definition/ con-20022540.

were consistent with an officer who had been through a traumatic incident and perceived feelings of lack of support from his administration.

Dr. Dodge sent a copy of that report to Dr. Campion, and I believe he sent a copy to my own Sheriff's administration. Since we were in the midst of a grievance, and because it was private medical information, there was no discussion directly with them. It was another situation of hurry up and wait from someone on the side of the Sheriff's administration. This time, I was told it was Dr. Campion who was delayed. And, of course, the Administrative Review of the shooting still wasn't complete. At least not to me or my attorney's knowledge. In my weekly meetings with the Undersheriff he brought up that things were building with rumors at the Patrol Station. I tried to reassure him that it wasn't me causing any of the ruckus but I could tell he didn't believe me. Each week in the Undersheriff's office he would let me vent and I would continuously stress my frustration with the duty assignments they kept giving me, the fact that they still hadn't gotten an official ruling on the Critical Incident Review, and that they had not received an official written report from Dr. Campion. Back in the days when he was a Patrol Lieutenant he would often vent about his frustrations, saying very unfavorable things about his bosses, so I thought I had a little safety in venting. I had to talk to someone. I later learned that I shouldn't have trusted him. I also noticed that the Sheriff seemed to be avoiding me. Originally I thought I was just being overly suspicious, but one day I was near his office talking to Commander Payne and I heard something behind me. I turned around and saw the Sheriff in slow motion, red faced, trying to quietly back away from me. He appeared to be trying to avoid me. I looked at him and said "Sheriff" in a welcoming manner. He looked at me and said, "Dustin" and then he walked quickly into his office through the Commander's office. I thought, "How petty of him!" I remained as positive and as quiet as I could be about everything, as my attorney requested. At this point, I'm not sure it helped, but I didn't want to give them any more ammo if we ended up in court.

Apparently the Critical incident review came through in July of 2004 but neither my union attorney nor I were officially notified. I learned of it only because it was noted in the "Referral Information" for the fitness-for-duty evaluation. That was fifteen months after the shooting and ten months after the official notice of the Administrative Review beginning. Remember, I was under an official order not to share the details of that incident with anyone not officially privileged to access it for ten months. By August of 2004 I had had enough of all this. Admittedly I had a couple of other outside stresses happen in October 2003 as my stepfather died from cancer and days later one of my best friends committed suicide, both of which happened about a month after my wedding. Because of those funerals and all of the time I took off when I felt stressed, I had used up all of my vacation and sick time, which meant I was getting less extra "stress days" off, as I called them. The "stress days" were simply me taking days off to get out of the office here or there, and away from the stress of the administration. As I built up days off for either sick days or vacation, I would use them. My therapist thought it was a good idea since it was keeping me as grounded as I could be in this situation.

One day I had an extra bad day. On this day, things had built up and I didn't have any days off left to take. It was a Friday so I had to have my normal "Friday meeting" with the Undersheriff. At least that meant it was almost the weekend and I could get away from this place. The conversation started with the normal superficial niceties. He asked how I was doing and I was honest and told him "not good." I shared, as I did every week, my frustrations with my duty assignments. By this time, I was sitting on my ass every day at Crime Lab doing practically nothing. It was in the basement of the main office building, with no windows and no way for me to run into normal staff. It appeared to me, and others in the department, that they were keeping me isolated from others by hiding me in the basement. I was also venting to the Undersheriff about the schedule they forced me on and how it created problems with my parenting schedule with my oldest son's mother. During our conversation I took a moment and laughed, shaking my head. He asked me what was up. I looked at him and said:

> *"Let's start with the fact that I don't believe in suicide. Period. And I've always questioned how in the hell any police officer could let their administration drive them so crazy that they eat their gun. And as much as I still want to question it, and I wouldn't do it myself, I now understand how an administration can drive an officer to suicide."*

I reiterated that I, in no way, was suicidal. But I meant what I said. I could now see and understand the stress levels which administrative staff can create. By telling him this, I hoped he would understand the kind of stress their procedures or failure to follow the established guidelines, created for officers. I was grasping at the slightest of hopes that they would give me some reprieve. Unfortunately, all I seemed to do was give them more ammo, which was used later to describe me as suicidal.

CHAPTER 14
UNDERSTANDING TRAUMA

I searched deeply to understand what was going on. Was I broken from the start as Dr. Campion had suggested? Or did the incident and the events that followed cause this? So, as much as I didn't like to read, I started reading and researching over the years following the shooting. I searched for my answers in books such as *CopShock: Surviving Posttraumatic Stress Disorder* by Allen R. Kates. I researched various websites and had discussions with other survivors. I did a tremendous amount of self-reflection. It was all incredibly eye-opening. Although both my therapist Penny and Dr. Gordy Dodge had diagnosed me with PTSD, I struggled with that label. Not so much because of embarrassment, but because when I acknowledged or said I had PTSD, I felt I was disrespecting soldiers and officers who had endured more violent encounters than mine.

To understand Post Traumatic Stress (PTS) and Post Traumatic Stress Disorder (PTSD) I had to do further research. Through that research, and my own therapy sessions, I understood much more. A traumatic event is defined as any event that has sufficient impact to overwhelm the usually effective coping skills of either an individual or a group. These events are typically sudden, emotionally powerful, and outside the range of usual human experience.

130

These events may have a strong emotional effect even on well-trained and experienced individuals. The book *CopShock*, as well as numerous other sites, outline that it's not something that is just happening to police and military, but those are the more commonly recognized demographics it occurs in. *Cop Shock* outlines that unmanaged suppressed feelings "have a way of exploding months or years after horrifying incidents, but facing these emotions immediately may prevent that from happening."[3] The first time I read that I had already had my outburst at the Patrol station. This behavior was not like me. Although I'm pretty direct, I'm normally pretty calm and tend to use humor instead of anger. Now I have a better understanding of why my behavior changed so drastically. It bothers me knowing that my department did not consider the effects of PTSD. It bothers me even more that Dr. Campion did not even consider it as a diagnosis, even though it was known at the time that behavior surrounding traumatic incidences and PTSD often mimic those of personality disorders.

I don't know at that time if this was understood, but more studies show that PTSD isn't so much about a single traumatic event for police officers, but instead it's often a cumulative effect of stress exposures on the job. The traumatic event seems to open the door. In the interview article, "Trauma On The Job: Why law enforcement officers suffer from PTSD, and what we can do about it" provided on Lexipol, a police training and policy website, Karen Lansing

---

[3] Kates, A.R. *CopShock: Surviving Posttraumatic Stress Disorder (PTSD)* (Tucson, AZ: HOLBROOK Street Press, 2001).

shares a better understanding of today's complexities with PTSD and the law enforcement field. Karen is a licensed psychotherapist and Diplomate of the American Academy of Experts in Traumatic Stress. In the article, she states that "although it's tempting to associate PTSD with a single incident...it is often caused by exposure to numerous traumatic incidents over several years or, in some cases, an entire career."[4] She continues that, "I typically see what we call cumulative PTSD, incidents involving shootings or improvised explosive devices will often open the door. It's easier for an officer to come in after one of those incidents because everyone understands that they should be talking about it. But the shooting or 'things that go bang' are just the latest incident sitting on top of a stack of other traumatic incidents."[4]

I suffered from PTSD, and I needed to accept that. Obviously I was no longer accepting of Dr. Campion's diagnoses' of Narcissistic and Histrionic Personality Disorders. Not just because I wanted to defend myself and be normal, but because it didn't make sense. I had passed two other psychological evaluations, one for Ramsey County and one three and a half years later for Anoka County, both of which were full pre-employment evaluations. I also did a shorter evaluation that was required to get into the Law Enforcement Skills Program in college. Dr. Campion put in his report that the other psychological evaluations were

---

[4] Lexipol, "Trauma On The Job: Why law enforcement officers suffer from PTSD, and what we can do about it." *Lexipol, 2016,* www.lexipol.com/news/trauma-on-the-job.

flawed in their results, and he said the same thing about Dr. Dodge's results, which was pretty convenient. Further research into the two personality disorders certainly outlined some behaviors I was displaying post shooting, but not pre-shooting. Dr. Dodge, who is an expert on traumatic incidences in law enforcement and in the military, including an expert on PTSD, gave me some better insight. Dr. Dodge explained that personality disorders outlined by Dr. Campion would have been present in late adolescence to early adulthood and "definitely prior to [my] previous psychological assessments for employment as a police officer." He explained, after review of his own testing as well as my previous evaluations and raw testing data, and said, "There's no indication of a personality disorder in that material."

It was quite a relief to have an expert say that. He explained to me, and in his official report:

> "Mr. Reichert does have some personality characteristics that can, and likely have, caused him some interpersonal difficulties, especially in relationship to with his supervisors. These include cockiness, outspokenness, and being quite outspoken. However these are not to a degree to constitute unfitness and at times provide him with self-assurance to effectively take command of situations when necessary."

That fits me pretty well. I tend to come across a little cocky and I can be outspoken at times. Those characteristics coupled with my sense of humor have also served me well both as an officer and in my current profession as an entertainer. They often came in handy in dealing with difficult people and making sometimes quick and tough decisions on duty. I've always considered them as an asset, especially as a police officer, and a part of my strength.

He went on to explain:

> *"...a dynamic that some evaluators are not aware of is that PTSD can display itself in some ways that are similar to certain personality disorder characteristics, including some of the above. What is also important to keep in mind is that after an officer involved shooting, if the officer perceives that he does not have administrative support and approval for his actions some mistrust, resentment, and irritability often occurs for a while, these ironically not always presenting the officer in the most favorable light".*

I'd say he nailed it. I was certainly feeling a complete lack of support from my Sheriff's administration, and had been for more than a year at that point. And it seemed they blocked me at every turn.

Dr. Dodge concluded:

> *"Mr. Reichert has experienced psychological effects from the shooting that should be recognized, and should continue to be addressed in therapy. If he continues in therapy, however, there is no indication that he cannot be returned to full duty, and in fact doing so will also be emotionally beneficial to him. I consequently conclude that, from a psychological*

*perspective, Mr. Reichert is fit to return to full duty as
a Deputy with the Anoka County Sheriff's
Department, and recommend that he be reinstated as
such."*

That was an emotional statement for me. I often felt
suspicious and almost paranoid, and then I would get mad at
myself for feeling that way. Having the official diagnosis, one
that fit and made overall sense, was redeeming, especially
since we had it on paper now. Three evaluations to Dr.
Campion's one. And the diagnosis of PTSD made far more
sense than the personality disorders, especially with
everything that had happened by now. Maybe, just maybe, I
could be a cop again. This didn't mean I was "normal" or
healed or had worked through everything I'd been going
through, I recognized that. But it was a relief anyway. I knew
that Dr. Dodge was officially clearing me for duty. Dr. Dodge
had told me that in his opinion I was fit for duty, but to see it
in writing gave me a real sense of relief. My excitement,
however, was short-lived.

CHAPTER 15
MEDICAL LEAVE OF ABSENCE

On Friday August 9, 2004, I was called up to the
Undersheriff's office. It was towards the end of the day but
not my normal time to meet, so I was surprised. I thought
maybe they finally had my written results of Dr. Campion's
fitness-for-duty evaluation. But I didn't trust him so I was also
wary. As I said earlier, they were well known among the staff
to deliver controversial news on Friday afternoon. It had
already happened earlier when they changed my
assignment to the administrative offices. But, once again, I
needed to try and stay calm and positive. As I approached
the Undersheriff's door, I could see that he, the Commander,
and our Human Resources Manager were sitting at his
conference table. The Human Resources Manager's
presence usually meant bad news, but three of them there
was a real cause for concern. I paused for a minute and
cautiously entered the room. I chuckled a moment and said,
"Looks like I need to contact my union attorney or at
minimum my union steward." I was reassured by all three
that wasn't necessary. I said, "So this isn't an official meeting
or punishment," and again they reassured me that it wasn't. I
knew something was up. They were lying to me. They
wouldn't even look me in the eyes. Their body movements
were stiff and guarded, with hesitation. They glanced at each
other's eyes far more than they focused on me. Undersheriff

King was stumbling over his words and I hadn't even sat down yet. Commander Payne had almost a hurt mothering look on her face. And the Human Resources Manager had a fake smile on her face, so I definitely knew this was bad. My heart raced and whatever was going to happen would happen, it's not like I could run away. So I looked at our Human Resources Manager and said, "Well, if it's not official then she can get the fuck out of here, because I don't want her in here!" That probably wasn't wise on my part, but every encounter with her after the shooting felt like a disaster. She froze with a shocked look on her face. She looked at the Undersheriff and he nodded at her and told her it was okay. She wouldn't even look at me as she left the room. That was probably one of the greatest feelings during all of this. I hate to be vengeful, but it felt good to see the shoe on the other foot for her, even if only for a brief moment.

I cautiously sat down at the table and they started talking. I don't think I heard much of what they were saying. My focus was on that piece of paper in front of them. It was upside down to me, but I'm good at reading upside down. I heard him say, "We know you're dealing with stress and family schedule issues, so we're going to put you on leave to help you manage that." As nice as he tried to make that sound, I could read the memo. It was titled "Notice of Administrative Leave Pending Fitness-For-Duty Evaluation." I saw words such as, "you are restrained," "at no time," and "no direct communication, direct or indirect." As he continued to talk, my heart was pounding like crazy and I heard nothing else he said. I read enough of the memo in front of him to know what was going on. After all the shitting on me, mistakes on their part, psychological evaluation crap, and now this, they were going to force me into a medical leave? At one point the memo was placed directly in front of me. I don't know if they handed it to me or I grabbed it. I continued to read it while they were talking. Then I got to the part on the memo where it said, "Our records indicate that you are currently issued two weapons…" and then it went on to list the models and serial numbers. I interrupted him and said, "You're taking my fucking guns?" I repeated statements such as, "I can't believe you guys are doing this to me. After all you've done to me already…now this?" They tried to comfort me but I refused to listen to their bullshit and attempts to comfort me.

Shortly after that I decided I was done with this conversation, especially without my union attorney present. I removed my gun from my holster, and removed the magazine and the round in the chamber to make the gun safe. I placed the gun, magazine, and chamber round on the table, attempting to get the taking of my gun out of the way, making it safe while I did so. But I didn't realize what I was doing in their eyes. They both jumped with a shocked expression on their faces. In hindsight I guess I can see how that sudden movement with the gun scared them, especially while delivering this kind of news, but I also didn't care at that point. And, although it was unintentional, I do chuckle about it when it comes up. Like I said earlier, I have to take my wins where I can, even if unintentional. I asked if they were taking my badge too and they said no. Shortly after I told them I was done with this conversation without my attorney present and I got up and left that office.

Sheriff Andersohn's office was attached directly to the Undersheriff's with a door in-between their offices as well as their own normal doors to the main area. As I walked out of the office, the Sheriff's door was closed, which meant he was in there, otherwise he leaves it open. I yelled out, "It would have been nice if you weren't such a coward and had at least told me yourself." I walked out of that office red faced with tears in my eyes. I kept those tears from falling until I got into the parking garage at least. Then I completely broke down. I probably sat out there crying in my vehicle for at least fifteen minutes. My emotions were now at an all-time high, and my career at an all-time low. My drive home was mostly a blur. I called my union attorney and she was already aware of the Medical Leave. She said we would use it as a part of our grievance process. She tried to comfort me and gave me some suggestions to keep busy over the weekend to calm my world. Admittedly she had been one of my rocks through the process at that point so her comfort and encouragement meant a lot. I told my wife on the way home and we tried to keep our weekend as busy and peaceful as possible. I didn't sleep much that weekend.

Eventually my union attorney found out from the County Attorney's office that the official reasoning was not for my family and children as the Sheriff's administration had claimed. They actually said the reasoning given to the County Attorney's Office was because I had been "rambling about suicide" and "snapping and unsnapping my gun." What? I was in complete shock. I couldn't believe the betrayal by the Undersheriff. And the lies! Besides the fact that he assured me it was okay to "vent," I did so since I had been prevented from talking to my peers. Not only did he use my trust against me, he completely distorted my conversation with him about suicide. It should have been clear I wasn't suicidal and if he really felt I was, then I would have thought he would have addressed that at the time or shortly after. It was obvious to my attorney and I that they were looking for a reason to get me on leave and out of their hair. Since they were still thinking I was stirring up my partners, this was a perfect way to get rid of me. But they were wrong. And their actions were based on those wrong assumptions, so the betrayal I felt was unbelievable. I kept thinking to myself, *Did they send me home on a Friday so I would commit suicide?* Inside I knew better, but it was convenient timing on their part. As for the snapping and unsnapping of the gun, I'm not sure what that is about. It is common for plain clothes officers to check to make sure their gun is holstered since we wear holsters with less security than street holsters. Maybe I was checking that without conscious thought while in his office. I certainly wasn't unsnapping it and Undersheriff King was definitely the type to call me out on it out loud. What made it worse was the fact that the memo I received also advised me:

"You are restrained from entering the Anoka County Sheriff's Offices non-public areas including the Patrol Station and Substations.

At no time are you to enter or remain in the Anoka County Sheriff's Offices during non-business hours.

You are to have no communication, direct or indirect, with any employee of the Anoka County Sheriff's

*Office unless it is of a social nature and has nothing
to do with work or any work-related matter."*

During that meeting with the Undersheriff and the
Commander, he said he would send a Sergeant to my house
to retrieve the other handgun issued to me. I told him that
neither his administration, nor a Sergeant officially
representing his administration was allowed at my house or
on my property. I told them to notify the Sergeant I would be
at the Patrol Station at a specific time to turn over my other
department issued duty handgun, which was different than
the plain clothes gun I had turned over to them earlier at the
meeting. The Sergeant they gave that "detail" to was
Sergeant Dave Sievert. The truth is, Sergeant Sievert drove
me nuts when I was a Patrol Deputy and he was constantly
a pain in the ass. I even tried to arrange my shift bids to
avoid him. But that day, and every time I've seen him since,
he was nothing but compassionate towards me. Years later I
shared with him what happened building up to that point and
how that day went down. He told me it was probably one of
the worst "detail" he had ever been assigned, especially
since he was left pretty much in the dark about it except to
take possession of my handgun.

I was in complete shock all weekend with many bouts of
crying, and then ready for the fight, only to go back to feeling
emotional and defeated. I was alive, but the administration of
my department, my fraternal family, had turned on me. I had
risked my life for my agency and in return I felt like they were
completely shutting me out, for political reasons that had
nothing to do with me directly. I was a pawn in their political
game; that much I was confident of. When I say political, I'm

referring to my feeling of the Sheriff and his administration making decisions that best fit them as individuals. The Sheriff to keep his reputation intact. The Undersheriff, and others, to keep in the good graces of the Sheriff and keep their career on track. I found out shortly after that a memo had been sent to all Patrol Deputies saying that they were ordered not to visit me on duty and not to discuss anything office related if they did interact with me. The way they treated me you would have thought I was involved in an illegal or criminal incident, not a clean, justifiable shooting. I was angry. Very angry. And I was not going to let them treat me that way. I needed to defend myself. This is where those personality traits outlined by Dr. Dodge would do me good. I made it clear to my union attorney that I wanted to put a full fight in. On August 23, 2004 we officially started the grievance process, focusing on "discipline without just cause." And, of course, the administration put up nothing but road blocks claiming that the leave of absence wasn't discipline. Each step of the way, they would wait until the last minute to respond, which significantly prolonged the process. By that time, I absolutely hated these fuckers.

We still hadn't gotten Dr. Campion's official written report. On September 15, after there had already been an extension on the grievance deadlines, I received a memo from the Undersheriff. Surprisingly he "offered" me an opportunity to be interviewed by Dr. Campion now that he had received all of Dr. Gordy Dodge's materials. The letter stated that Dr. Campion did not feel it was necessary to personally interview me. My union attorney sent the County Attorney's Office a pretty scathing letter outlining the huge flaws in Dr.

Campion's Process, the lack of related credentials by Dr. Liaboe, the lack of report, and only a verbal summary to the administration and the fact that this was contrary to three previous psychological reports, one recent and two pre-employment that say there were no personality disorders. The attorney also pointed out that both Dr. Campion and Dr. Liaboe missed the PTSD diagnosis. She further stated the Undersheriff appeared to be attempting to influence the grievance process when he sent me the memo "offering" me a meeting with Dr. Campion, especially since Dr. Campion had already indicated it was not necessary to speak directly to me.

We were scheduled for Mediation later that fall. As part of the process I wrote a letter to the Undersheriff requesting that they provide a copy of my psychological evaluation to my attorney. When she finally got it, it was dated October 5, 2004, which was seven months after the evaluation. To this day I am still dumbfounded how the Sheriff, an intelligent man, could stand so strongly behind such a flawed process, a Dr. who is giving verbal results over the phone for psychological evaluations, a Dr. who never met the person they were evaluating and didn't think it was necessary, a Dr. who took seven months to complete a written report, a Dr. who didn't provide a written report until after he got the report from my independent Dr. with a diagnosis of PTSD who had tested me after Dr. Campion's test date.

As upset as I was, the receiving of the official written report from Dr. Campion really opened up some information we were searching for and confirmed some of my suspicions. It was confirmed that the "Reason for Referral" was

"Independent Psychological Examination" and was requested by our Resources Manager. This is what the "Statement of Problem" from our HR Manager, said:

Deputy Reichert was referred for an Independent Psychological Examination with regard to his readiness for duty after a suspect was shot on 05/13/03 as a result of a loud music complaint. The victim came to the door with a gun, and Deputy Reichert shot him twice. The victim responded by shooting Deputy Reichert two times. As a result, Deputy Reichert was hospitalized and off of work until July 21, 2003. The internal investigation of the shooting has not been completed. Deputy Reichert has been cleared by a grand jury. The sheriff's department has some questions with regards to the shooting and there is also concern with Deputy Reichert's response after the shooting. The shooting was eventually determined in July of 2004 to be within the confines of the departmental policy and state statutes. It appears he demanded an inordinate amount of attention, and demanded medals and other recommendations. He filed a civil suit against the victim, and the victim's family responded with a civil suit. Deputy Reichert subsequently dropped his civil suit. There is concern that Deputy Reichert made several references to the victim, Erik D. Nylen, as being a "bastard" and "asshole" and "the guy who tried to rob my son of a father." There is concern that Deputy Reichert does not express remorse over the shooting and does not appear to have feelings of

*emotion or empathy for the death of Mr. Nylen.
According to the referral information, he references
the fact that he had "gone into battle" and "won" by
beating the "bad guy." At one point, Deputy Reichert
gave an "emotional" dissertation about him and
Deputy Samantha Cruze not receiving awards for
their action that resulted in the death of Mr. Nylen. It
was also reported that Deputy Reichert was in such
pain with his arm afterward, that he rolled around on
the floor crying, which caused his [6]-year-old son to
be quite upset.*

Wow! When I read that I was floored. My blood boiled higher
than I thought possible. I read it a few times thinking it had to
be a mistake or I had read it wrong. I recalled back to the
day when I was asked to submit to a psychological
evaluation and how I had asked if it was because of my
outburst. Both my Human Resources Manager and the
Undersheriff assured me it had nothing to do with my
outburst and instead, it was because I was in a shooting and
a standard procedure. But they lied or, at minimum, they
weren't completely honest. The "information" shared in her
memo is either grossly exaggerated or taken totally out of
context. I don't recall making the statements they claim I
made about Erik Nylen, but it is possible they were part of
my outburst at Patrol, including the comments about going
into battle. I'm not sure. I'll admit I was pretty heated that day
and my stress had built up. I felt like I had been in self-
preservation mode defending myself against my own
administration. I had gone into battle during one of the
simplest of calls. I have two bullet holes to prove it. So in the

midst of dealing with the actions and inactions of my administration, I was still trying to deal with the shooting. Both consumed more of my mind and emotions than I had to offer. I was confused, curious, and even angry over the shooting. And it's possible I may have even called Mr. Nylen a bastard. This should have been a simple noise call where we would simply tell him to turn down the music and be on our way. No conflicts, no arrests, no tickets, and certainly no deaths. What was he thinking? How is it possible he didn't recognize us as Police Officers on that full moonlit night? Why didn't he listen to the commands? At the same time I was struggling to deal with my own injuries and my own mortality. I hadn't had the time to figure out how I felt toward him. No matter how justified I was in shooting him, I still relived the ordeal over and over, mostly trying to understand it all.

I guess I should have been surprised by the statements they said I had made during the outburst, but I wasn't. Not too much was surprising me at this point when it came to my administration. The truth is, I didn't have any feelings of anger towards Erik Nylen. I'll never know why he did what he did, but it happened and now it was over. In reality, I don't believe I ever had an opportunity to fully, if even partially, process the Erik Nylen part of the shooting. I can tell you where I stand now though. Erik Nylen paid the ultimate price for his actions and there is no point in feeling angry toward him or his actions. I can't ask him to pay a larger price than he already has. My anger was towards the Sheriff and his administration. What REALLY stuck out in the referral information was the comment about the Sheriff's Office having "some questions regarding the shooting." I can't be sure exactly what that meant, but I knew it meant he was continuing to question whether Erik Nylen was going to shoot me or not. Shame on those in administration who questioned Mr. Nylen's intent! I know it is their job to question the actions of their officers and keep everyone accountable, but this was a clearly a justifiable shooting from the start and I had done exactly as I had been trained. Nothing is worse than Monday morning quarterbacking of an incident from your fully lighted, comfortable, safe office. What questions could you have when a gun is pointed between your Deputy's eyes from such a close distance? The answer should have been none. I can see why the poor family of Erik Nylen would question anything and everything, but not the man who carries the same badge, has patrolled the same streets, and been involved in the same training programs.

I was shocked about the civil suit information, or should I say the mis-information. It's true, I did have an attorney exploring the idea of a lawsuit against the Estate of Eric Nylen. This was during a time of great anger. In the attorney's exploration, against my explicit instructions, he actually did file the law suit. He was only supposed to explore the viability at that point. After he filed I got very upset with him and demanded that he drop the suit shortly thereafter. And contrary to the information provided in the referral, the family never did file a suit against me, the office or the county. They, too, had been exploring the idea of a civil suit against me and my department, but prior to my attorney filing my suit in error. I remember hearing how upset the Sheriff was when it happened and I tried to explain to him that the attorney filed against my wishes, but the Undersheriff wouldn't listen. Regardless, that wasn't the Sheriff's business if I did or did not utilize my right to seek civil compensation for my injuries from the Estate of Erik Nylen.

While I was out on forced medical leave, I was required to make weekly phone calls on Tuesdays and Fridays to Undersheriff King at 9:00 a.m. Each week I made sure it was a prompt call as I didn't want there to be any more reasons for them to target me. As the summer and fall went on, the calls weren't even answered and I had to leave voicemails. For the most part, that was better because my hatred for him at that point was almost more than my hatred for the Sheriff. On November 22, 2004 I was finally notified that the phone calls were no longer necessary, which was a relief because I hated making them and the Undersheriff usually didn't answer anyway.

In December, 2004, I was having a strategy meeting with my union attorney, Marylee Abrahams. We met at the Chipotle in Coon Rapids, MN. By this time, I greatly trusted her and she had taken this case somewhat personal. She had a good strategy brewing. She was in the middle of describing the strategy and I liked it. We planned on arranging another fitness-for-duty evaluation from a third evaluator, which both sides agreed to. She felt that the likelihood of "passing" it was high and then we would have four evaluations to their one. Then I stopped for a minute and looked out of the window we were sitting by. She asked if something was wrong. I paused for a minute and felt pure fear, anger, and self-pity. It was a feeling I had previously only felt right after the shooting, and then again right after they said I had "failed" the fitness-for-duty evaluation. I slowly looked up at her and said, "What if I don't want to do this anymore?" She asked me exactly what I meant. I said I felt confident I was going to win this, but then what? The Sheriff would still detest me and target me, probably even more so, especially since I would have beaten him. As I looked back out of the window, I knew the grievance win would be held against me. I knew I would be likely stuck in the courts as a bailiff until his term as Sheriff was up, and who knows how the next Sheriff after that would handle it. I knew I would wither like a dying flower working in the courts. I'm a street cop. I'm a drug cop. I'm a people cop. I had seen so many police officers in their later years turn pessimistic and attitudes turn bad, often because of the pathway their careers took them. I couldn't let myself wither up like that.

As I sat there looking out of the window, I thought about all the wonderful opportunities I'd had in my short career – more than many police officers will have in their entire careers. I knew that I had done good work, and made an impact, which is what most police officers desire when they enter Law Enforcement. I didn't want to fight any more. I was tired and stressed. I didn't want the Sheriff to win, but I wanted out. I felt I could still walk away with pride, while I was at the height of my career, rather than returning to a support role that didn't suit me. I finally looked back up at Marylee and said again, "What if I don't want to do this anymore? Seriously, what if I don't want to fight anymore? What if I want to be done? What are my options?" She didn't try to push me either way and said she would support whatever decision I made. I didn't say much else during the rest of the meeting. We agreed she would make contact with the County Attorney and the Sheriff and find out what options were available to me.

CHAPTER 16
SETTLEMENT AND MOVING ON

I was surprised when I heard back from my union attorney. She said the Sheriff already had a settlement offer available. My suspicions were confirmed at that point…the Sheriff wanted me gone. It didn't hurt as much as I thought it might. I was starting to become numb with their actions and lack of actions. We reached a settlement that was acceptable to me. As with everything else going on in this process, they changed things around after we had an agreement, making changes after we agreed, but before it was on paper and signed. Regardless, I was ready to move on. I was struggling with my arm more than I was admitting. As the numbness faded and as the nerves healed, I was struggling with more pain and weakness than expected. This was especially true with lifting and throwing. I noticed it more when playing darts and throwing footballs with my son. It was time to move on as I now wanted to concentrate on my physical and emotional healing.

I went back to my Orthopedic Surgeon and shared my update and symptoms. After a long meeting, he told him that he felt my desire to retire was a good decision as he was worried about my safety with my arm limitations. Our retirements are handled by Public Employee Retirement Association (PERA) and they required an independent evaluation. I was suspicious of everything and everyone at that point who obviously weren't on my side, so I went into it with a bad attitude and suspicious because I had no idea how much of a fight it might be. Although I understood this was independent, because of the previous situation with the fitness-for-duty evaluation, I didn't know what my administration had told the PERA doctor. However, I also felt the Sheriff wanted me gone, so I didn't know what to expect. After a detailed evaluation, he also came to the conclusion that I could no longer safely perform the duties of a Deputy Sheriff. On March 22, 2005 I was officially approved by PERA for retirement disability benefits.

On May 2, 2005 I turned in my resignation. The one stipulation I had was that I wanted my work family (my partners) at the Anoka County Sheriff's Office to hear the news directly from me, not via an impersonal memo in their mailbox. Of course, my administration didn't agree to fearing I would cause more of a ruckus. But that wasn't my intent at all. These were my brothers and sisters of the badge. I had been forced to hide information from them for almost two years and they deserved to hear the news directly from me. The administration put up every block that they could. I would have preferred to hold the meeting at the Sheriff's Office but in the beginning they refused.

So with the help of my union steward we arranged it as an emergency union meeting held at a local church. The administration responded by prohibiting anyone from attending while on duty. After a bunch of back and forth messages, I finally I asked my union attorney to call and plea for them to back off. I asked her to convince them that they were going to have to take my word for it that there were no malicious intentions. I asked her to tell them it would be better to do it this way because a memo would likely ignite the other Deputies more than before. Finally, they hesitatingly agreed to allow the meeting to take place at the Patrol office, but only if I agreed that Undersheriff King could be present. I didn't care if he or the Sheriff were present but I told them in no way would I allow our Human Resources Manager to be present or involved.

A Patrol-wide message went out on staff pagers advising that Deputy Reichert had an important announcement to make just before roll call that day, which was May 3, 2005. I arrived at Patrol a little before and it was a strange feeling since I hadn't been there for over a year. It was my home in the department and it felt good to be there, even if it was the last time. They asked if I wanted to clean out my locker, but given the previous actions by the administrations, I had cleaned it out over a year ago. To avoid potentially disruptive individual conversations, I hid in the Sergeant's office until it was time for the meeting to start. My Union Steward, Deputy Dave Wiley, was amazing. He was one of the first people there when I first got shot; he was there at many of the portions in between; he was there helping me fight to get this notification approved at the Patrol station; and he was there that day. And he didn't leave my side throughout all of it.

A few minutes before my announcement, I had stepped out of the Sergeant's office into the hall. I saw so many people, so many Deputies...my partners....my friends...my family. I had to jump back into the Sergeant's office for a couple minutes to find my composure. My emotions hit me like a baseball bat. A flood of feeling honor, sadness, anxiety, relief and more hit me all at once. I took a deep breath and wiped away the tears that were about to roll out of my eyes. I entered the patrol room red-faced and looked at a packed room full of my brothers and sisters of the badge, many friends, and many new faces, all with questioning and concern on their faces. And the Undersheriff was in the back of the room. What an absolute honor that so many people had turned up to hear my announcement. After taking one more deep breath, I spoke:

"Thank you guys so much for coming on such short notice. I have some important things that I want to share with you and I want to ask you to listen. I've been on quite a journey with the shooting and because of the legal battles I was unable to share a lot with you, my friends and my partners. So it was important to me today that I share this with you personally. Although my healing has significantly improved, I haven't been completely honest about the level of my pain and some concerns with the damage to my arm. Effective today, May 3, 2005, I have offered my resignation to Sheriff Andersohn and he has accepted it. I know you guys are going to be suspicious and think that I was forced by the administration, but honestly this was my decision. I have truly loved being a Deputy Sheriff with the Anoka County Sheriff's Office. And I am proud to say that I wore this badge and worked next to many of you. And I will go on cherishing that."

I struggled to say it as clear as I would have liked, as I got choked up. However, even though my speech was broken, they heard me. I found it interesting to see the look on the Undersheriff's face standing in the back of the room. I don't know if my emotions got to him, or maybe he felt bad for what had happened to me, most of it at his hand. Maybe it's because he thought he might get strung up by a room full of angry Deputies. I'll never know. I received lots of love and hugs and good wishes after the announcement. Then I made my way out of the Patrol station for the last time ever. At my request, a bunch of us met at Buffalo Wild Wings that night and had a little going away/retirement party. I will forever cherish the love they all gave me on such short notice.

DEPUTY DUSTIN REICHERT (RET)

PART 3
Time to Heal

CHAPTER 17
MENDING MY WOUNDS

The beginnings of my healing began right after I was told I had "failed" my original fitness-for-duty evaluation. I had accepted the verbal results, at least initially, that had been given to me by the Sheriff. I knew, because of the shooting, that the county would pay for some therapy, especially since I hadn't yet had a chance to process the attempted taking of my life or taking the life of another. As I said earlier, I had hoped going to a therapist would be on my terms but realistically I'm not sure it would ever truly have been "on my terms," regardless of the follow-up actions from my administration. Either way, it was best to go see someone in light of this new information and verbal diagnosis. Our Human Resources Manager got me a couple of names of therapists and, after my insistence, they specialized in dealing with police officers. They were both a part of the St. Paul Police Employee Assistance Program (EAP); a great program primarily funded by St. Paul Police Department for officers dealing with traumatic incidences. The St. Paul program required that a St. Paul Police Officer involved in a critical incident, defined as a serious injury or death, meets with an EAP representative immediately after the incident. Then within forty-eight hours the officer would meet with a professional, and within seventy-two hours there would be a general meeting with the individual and other law enforcement personnel. This program was also made available to Police Officer's statewide. I wish my administration would have taken advantage of the program at the beginning and then maybe we would have avoided this two-year conflict.

Out of the two names given to me, I chose a woman named Penny. I was familiar with the male name on the list and he was part of a gang research program I had been a part of prior to coming to Anoka County. It was obviously better the person was unconnected from me. Plus, I felt more comfortable with a woman at this point. I can't explain why, it was just my feeling. Maybe it was a motherly thing. Who knows? Since I'm not big on the idea of going to "head doctors" I wanted the decision to feel as comfortable as possible. I wasn't fond of the idea of someone poking around in my head, but I knew I had to move forward with healing. I mean, I had killed someone and they had tried to kill me. Although I didn't feel any real ill feelings about taking a life, I knew deep down inside I probably needed to address it, especially since I had moments of anger about him nearly leaving my son fatherless.

During my first session with Penny, at first I was standoffish. I wanted to share my pain and frustration but I also didn't trust anyone. Penny was very calm and had a relaxing demeanor, which made her great at opening me up. We did a few sessions and there was a good connection and she built my trust. It felt wonderful and calming to finally be able to open up to someone and not worry about judgment or retribution. And she seemed to have a genuine desire to help me to help myself. She often spoke of me having PTSD and she wanted to address that specifically. I hadn't been to Dr. Dodge at this point, so this was the first discussion about PTSD and I wasn't sure how I felt about it. My mind was still so scrambled I wasn't sure if I did or did not have PTSD. Mostly that's because I didn't understand exactly what it was. But as time went by and I learned more about it, I began to understand that I had it.

One day she mentioned a treatment for PTSD she thought might be helpful. It is called Eye Movement Desensitization and Reprocessing (EMDR). That sounded scary to me, almost like voodoo, and I told her I wasn't interested in anything like hypnosis. This is funny to me now, because years later I became a hypnotist and realized how non-voodoo and how helpful hypnosis really is! Penny reassured me it wasn't like that. As I mulled over the idea, I mentioned it to one of my close friends and partners who was also dealing with a different severe trauma involving a death from a crash he was in. I knew her personality would match his so I suggested it to him. To my surprise he started seeing her professionally. And even more surprising was the fact he did the EMDR treatment first, because he was looking for something to relieve his own pain. After his EMDR treatment he raved to me about its effects so I eventually agreed to go through it myself. A further research online showed that EMDR was a very effective method of helping to treat PTSD.

Basically, EMDR involves you looking at the facilitator's finger as she passes it back and forth over thirty times. She had me start out with an image in my mind related to something that was frustrating me. Then when I had that image locked in, she moved her finger back and forth repeatedly at different speeds. Periodically she stopped and asked me if it was the same image or different, and if different, and if I was willing to share, to share it. I don't know how long it went on, but it was certainly interesting. I started out with an image of the gun being pointed at my face and by the end of the session I had images related to the shooting, to other traumatic calls in my career, to the recent suicide of a good friend of mind, and to other incidents from my youth days. The things that popped into my mind were crazy. I'm not interested in sharing the details here, but when I was about eight years old I had been molested by an adult stranger at a community pool. I had never told anyone before and hadn't thought about it much after my teen years. When that image popped into my mind in that first session, it hit me strongly and I became emotional and started crying. Although Penny originally told me I didn't have to share the images with her, she asked that I share that particular one. After she had calmed me down, she wound down the session for the day.

Penny made me arrange ahead of time for a ride home after the session. I thought it was stupid I had to and that I would be fine. But sure enough, I was completely exhausted that afternoon and into the evening. Apparently, the basic premise of EMDR is about desensitizing the images and increasing the blood flow in areas they don't normally flow. Another way she described it is that it's like having all kinds of "stuff" locked in your short-term memory, and by doing the EMDR process you allow that "stuff" to be downloaded to your long-term memory, relieving your short-term memory.

The EMDR Institute Inc. more officially defines mental trauma healing and using EMDR to aid in that healing. This is an overview description of how EMDR and the healing mind work together:

EMDR (Eye Movement Desensitization and Reprocessing) is a psychotherapy that enables people to heal from symptoms and emotional distress that are the result of disturbing life experiences. Repeated studies show that by using EMDR people can experience the benefits of psychotherapy that once took years to make a difference. It is widely assumed that severe emotional pain requires a long time to heal. EMDR therapy shows that the mind can, in fact, heal from a psychological trauma much the way the body recovers from a physical trauma. When you cut your hand, your body works to close the wound. If a foreign object or repeated injury irritates the wound, it festers and causes pain. Once the block is removed, healing resumes. EMDR therapy demonstrates that a similar sequence of events occurs with the mental processes. The brain's information processing system naturally moves toward mental health. If the system is blocked or imbalanced by the impact of a disturbing event, the emotional wound festers and can cause intense suffering. Once the block is removed, the healing resumes.[5]

---

[5] EMDR Institute, Inc. "What is EMDR?," *EMDR Institute, Inc., 2016,* www.emdr.com/what-is-emdr.

By the second session of EMDR I was feeling tremendously less stressed and tense. That, mixed with weekly sessions of therapy, helped me to work through all the stresses and emotions of the last few months. Penny was a God send for me. She helped me reach the point where I could manage the ongoing PSTD symptoms on my own, allowing me to manage my life and relationships much more effectively and calmly.

It is interesting the kinds of things that help healing. During the summer for some reason mowing my lawn was therapeutic for me. I had a riding lawn mower so I could still mow my own lawn. It was one of the few things I could do around my house that summer. There was something about the fresh smell of the cut grass and keeping the lawn looking green. I thought I was a little crazy for doing it, but when I mentioned it to Penny she said it was a common stress reliever for many of her patients suffering from PTSD. That knowledge alone seemed to help me feel like I was finding some normality and sanity. Penny encouraged me to continue to take the sick and vacation days as needed and allowed since they were helping me. Of course, taking time off was raising red flags with my administration because I would take the days as soon I earned them. The administration viewed it as attendance abuse and turned it into me appearing to have problems instead of seeing it for what it was, which was a symptom of their treatment. But it was vital for handling my emotional stress and anger, especially in the later times of this fight, so I took time off as I needed. The stress revolving around my situation at the Sheriff's office started to increase so high that even the EMDR and general therapy weren't working as well anymore. I felt like I would take two steps forward, only to be knocked back three steps, so taking time off, as soon as I could, was the only additional thing which seemed to help.

When I was put on the later forced Medical Leave of Absence, I was probably at the peak of my stress levels. I had been suppressed emotionally, hidden from my partners, and couldn't talk to anyone. I felt like I had been treated with shame, lied about, deceived, and more, all by my Sheriff and his administration, who had left me feeling betrayed, which created overwhelming stress. I wasn't contemplating suicide or anything like that. That being said, I was starting to develop physical symptoms related to the stress, including breathing issues, shortness of breath, and eventually locking jaw issues where my jaw would lock and pop, causing tremendous headaches. I had been to my doctor for the breathing problems and, thinking it was asthma, tried different inhalers but none of them worked. Then my doctor did some additional tests and said he didn't think the inhalers were working because the problem was likely stress and anxiety related. As much as I hated to admit it, that made a lot of sense. Since I didn't have a history of anxiety, he prescribed taking one half to one full pill of antihistamine. I filled the prescription and tried a half pill dose once, but it made me so drowsy and rendered me so ineffective, I stopped taking them. I also went to a TMJ specialist for the locking jaw problems but the treatment plan was a pretty time intensive process and I already was at constant doctor and therapy appointments, so I put that part of the treatment off.

Once I understood it was more stress related, I knew I had to work on calming myself down. I shared this with my therapist and she helped me to develop some techniques to calm my stress levels down and it helped. The breathing and locking jaw symptoms came and went over the next ten plus years based on different stressors along the way but the symptoms became easier to manage. Today the breathing issue is completely under control and hasn't shown up for over a year. Although the jaw problems have gotten better overall, I finally returned to the TMJ specialist in 2016. I'm so glad I did. With a custom mouth guard at night and simple massage techniques I have had amazing results in calming the problem down.

CHAPTER 18
UNEXPECTED PATH TO DEEPER HEALING

Five months after I was shot, I married my fiancé, Stacy. We had already been planning the wedding for over a year and both agreed we had no interest in postponing it. There was all the normal stresses of planning a wedding, but after what we had been through, the wedding stress wasn't too bad. The greatest stressor was sexual related because the bullet that hit my pelvic region rendered me unable to have sex until it healed up. I was nervous about that for my wedding night. Luckily though, my wound healed up prior to that and I had full function back. And, one of my highlights is that, while on our honeymoon, we conceived a child who was born later that next year. And then another child four years later. My manhood was restored.

The first year of marriage was tough on us. I was in the middle of fighting Anoka County while continuing to work on my healing, all with the hopes of returning to be the one thing I loved to be...a Police Officer. I am told it is normal for the first year of marriage to be filled with many exciting moments and moments of stress. We already had a full plate of stress with the shooting and fighting for my career. To add to all that, shortly after my wedding my stepdad died of cancer. He helped to raise me from the time I was about eight. He and my mom divorced after I became a Deputy and we lost track of each other for a few years until he reached out to me through a mutual friend when he knew he was nearing the end of his life. I appreciated having such an influential part of my life back, even if for such a short time. After being reconnected, I spent the next couple of weeks enjoying as much time as possible with him and said goodbye to him. Then, days after his untimely death, one of my best friends committed suicide. We had been friends since high school and he had attended my wedding over a month earlier. You could say, at that time, stress was my first, middle, and last name. And, of course, we added a pregnant wife to the chaos. But my therapist Penny did a good job of helping keep things calm and organized in my head. As much as could be at least at that time. I remembered feeling a little inspired after reading *Visions of Courage: The Bobby Smith Story* by Dr. Bobby E. Smith. Dr. Smith was medically retired as a Trooper with the Maryland State Police. He had been in a shooting incident in 1986 where he was shot in the face, and ultimately blinded by his injuries. I had purchased the book from him when I met him while he was the Keynote Speaker for my DEA Academy I attended the year before I was shot. I finally got around to reading his book while trying to understand my own personal struggles. I figured if Dr. Smith could find positive light after the smoked had cleared, then I should be able to.

My therapist, Penny, left the St. Paul Employee Assistance Program and merged her practice with one in the southern Twin Cities. I went for a few sessions at her new location for some follow-up therapy and EMDR, but ultimately it was too difficult to make the forty-five minute drive on a regular basis.

I wasn't interested in trying to connect with a new therapist so I stopped therapy and stopped seeing Penny. For the most part, I felt I was at a plateau of my level of therapy driven healing. I felt like I moved on after that. I had been retired for a while now. Family life was getting somewhat normal. The primary stress would occur around the anniversary of the shooting, which was also the day before my birthday each year. Overall, each year was getting easier to deal with. I joked that I had two birthdays now, back to back. One on the day I survived the shooting and had given birth to a second chance at life, and of course my original birthday. But I also joked that I will be drunk for those three anniversary days, the day before the shooting, the shooting day, and my actual birthday.

The reality for many of those years is that I was drunk for those three days. Certainly not the best choice given the alcohol and addiction issues in my family. But I did feel the "need" to be drunk on those dates. I'm a pretty friendly drunk and don't get negative or aggressive in my drunk emotions so nobody questioned it, at least not directly to me. Then my excuses for drinking broadened and I would have a drink every time stress came up in my life. It spiraled fairly quickly. Before I knew it, I was drinking frequently, almost every night, sometimes even during the day. I would stay home and help make sure my kids were set with dinner and in bed. But once they were tucked in I would run out the door to go and join a poker game, smoke some cigars, and get my drink on. That, of course, led to many drunken nights of spending way too much money and making many poor decisions. By this time, I had purchased an entertainment company. Among the entertainment options my company offered, one was a karaoke DJ for bar shows. And I ran a very rowdy, alcohol driven bar show for a couple of bars. I was given the task of boosting the party on the nights I worked and to help increase alcohol sales. That was easy as long as they provided me with a reasonable bar tab. Reasonable went from two to three drinks to in excess of eight drinks, at times heavily poured shots. This led me back to way too many nights of driving home drunk, way too many hangovers, and way too many blackouts.

I often drove home drunk at night, which was against my strong moral base, especially for a Deputy who used to be one of the top DWI enforcers in my department. And the fact that over a decade before I had lost my brother Chad when he was eighteen after he got drunk and crashed his car. I felt guilty every morning I woke up after drinking too much and driving home drunk. This was especially true for the nights I blacked out and didn't remember driving home. My behavior was far from appropriate, and far from the top DWI enforcer that I used to be. I also cheated on my wife. I definitely felt like I was at a low point in my life. Finally I came clean to my wife about the indiscretions. It wasn't easy, but Stacy and I somehow worked our way through it. I pulled way back on the alcohol consumption and stayed home much more for the next few months. But once I felt like I had control of myself and my behavior, I started drinking heavily again.

Finally, in 2014 I quit working the bar shows. One bar I worked in had closed, and for the other I taken a break to run the music for my sons Varsity Football games. The pay was much less, but my drinking dropped significantly, almost

170

to zero, which meant my wallet also wasn't affected as negatively. I enjoyed the feeling of having no hangover in the mornings and I felt a lot healthier. I drank more water and even ate healthier. I started working out with the T25 program and eating better, and I even lost 25 lbs. I felt better, my back was better, my breathing was wonderful, and I could manage the lock jaw issues.

In September 2013 I was hired by the Minnesota Sheriff's Association (MSA) to be a Keynote Speaker for a conference. They wanted me to provide a program I was developing called "The Power of the Mind Series" with customizable content. Since the overall theme of the conference was mental health they also wanted me to discuss my incident, PTSD, and my pathway to recovery. I was nervous about this since I didn't feel comfortable saying I had it, much less talking about it. But I had already signed the contract so I was committed. Then I found a path to further my peace of mind in a place I hadn't expected. By this time the Sheriff had long been retired. James Stuart, my confidant during the chaos and now friend, had worked his way up the ranks within the department. When Sheriff Andersohn retired, James ran for and won his election as Sheriff of Anoka County. He had been the new Sheriff for a while and I called him to let him know about the speaking engagement for the Sheriff's Association and asked for his support. He knew the contact I was dealing with at the MSA and said, "You have my support, Dustin." I told him I wanted to be clear and said, "They want me to talk about the shooting incident, Jim," to which he calmly replied, "I know, that's okay." I told him, "I'm gonna tell the truth… you know, all of it." He said he understood and told me to use common sense in what I said. We both paused and then he said to me:

"Dustin. It happened. And our department made some mistakes and we learned from them hopefully. I, for one, learned a lot from your shooting. And should such an incident happen again with our department, things would go a lot differently."

I thanked him and we finished our conversation with light general talk.

When I hung up the phone I sat there at my desk in silence, tears welling up in my eyes. And then the tears started to flow. I didn't fully understand why at first. It felt good to finally get some support from the administration of the Anoka County Sheriff's Office. But it was more than that. I continued to cry for almost an hour before I finally shook away the emotions. After that I felt a sense of relief. Then I realized this was the first time anyone official from the Anoka County Sheriff's Office had acknowledged that the department had made mistakes. It wasn't about being right or wrong for me, as I had made mistakes too. But to know that someone official had acknowledged that mistakes were made department wide, opened up the door for true healing. I guess I finally felt vindicated.

I went into that speaking event feeling great. That speaking event and those I have done since have been a big part of my healing too. There are details and emotions that were pretty unorganized, and I wish I had brought a more organized presentation to the attendees, but they got the benefit of seeing me raw, unpolished, and real. I'm guessing there is a unique value to that as well. As a very personal and special part of that first speaking event, Deputy Samantha Cruze, my partner on the night of the shooting, attended. She had left Anoka County a few years back, but had re-entered Law Enforcement as a Deputy Sheriff down in Fillmore County in Southern, MN. When the Sheriff of her new agency heard I was speaking, he was kind enough to allow her to attend. He had heard about my presentation at the last minute and bent over backwards to rearrange schedules so she could attend. He did that for her, but he'll never know how special that was for me, too. When I introduced her at the very end, I choked up. But in a different way. I choked up with pride. Because my friend, my partner, my protector was there.

When Sheriff Stuart later discussed this book, he had an interesting perspective. He asked if it was negative against the agency. I said no, there are sections that are more negative towards certain individuals in the previous administration, but they were all truths based on the real actions of those individuals. His response was, "I don't care if you even write bad about me, I just hope you don't make the Anoka County Sheriff's Office look bad." So I hope I've written this book in a manner that portrays that. And if it doesn't, make no mistake. I LOVE the Anoka County Sheriff's Office. I am PROUD to have served my community with that ACSO badge on my chest and patch on my side. And I continue to love this amazing agency. And Sheriff

Stuart is a huge part of why the department continues to be an amazing department.

CHAPTER 19
FINALLY TELLING MY STORY IN THIS ANTI-POLICE CULTURE

After the acknowledgement by the new Sheriff Stuart, my previous confidant and friend, and the ability to finally speak publicly about the shooting and the aftermath, I had interesting conversations with many people. When I spoke to people, the story was always too filled with chaos to tell it in one sitting and have them clearly understand. Over the years I have been encouraged by different people to put the story on paper and share it. I thought about it for years, and even tried to start writing it at various times over the years, but I didn't know if it was right to do so or not. And I didn't know how to write it or structure it. I couldn't organize it in my own head, so how the hell was I going to organize it on paper? And I wasn't sure if anyone outside of Law Enforcement would even want to read my story. I was confident that officers would read it, but I didn't know whether the public or even police administrators would find value in it. And I worried, thinking that if I wrote this book, I was confirming Dr. Campion's personality diagnosis of narcissism. I remember a friend telling me that I shouldn't let Dr. Campion win. He said that people would want to hear my story and he thought it might help others, and maybe help remind police administrators of the damage they can do in such delicate situations. So in 2014, I started organizing my thoughts and writing my story.

The writing began. And as I typed the words they flowed easily, at least in the beginning. I smiled and enjoyed the process as I wrote about life and history and my journey to being a Police Officer. As you can imagine, writing about the shooting brought forth some tension and tears. But amazingly I didn't get too emotional. Overall, I think I had healed from that. By accepting the shooting, by re-evaluating it in my head many times prior, and by letting go of any anger towards Mr. Nylen, I was able to heal. But, as I wrote the third section of this book, it became a lot tougher. I had to take breaks to research more information, but most of my breaks were emotional. I reached a point where my jaw would pop and lock like crazy. And I found myself staying up until all hours trying to work on it. This all led to me being crabby and snippy and I almost quit writing permanently over it as it didn't feel right for my healing. But after a two-week break, I started writing again. I knew it was important for me to get through it and to continue organizing it all in my head. And I'm glad I did, because when the rough draft was complete I went through the emotions and returning to writing made it a lot easier on me.

After having a few trusted people read the original draft I received a lot of good feedback and encouragement to move forward with this in order to eventually get it published. I was encouraged to add a few more fun stories from my days on the street, which was fun. And a good hypnotist friend of mine who read it reminded me of the culture of misunderstanding of police and the anti-police rhetoric and felt this was a good time to share my experience. I had already felt the same thing but I didn't know if my thinking was on target.

Each stage of this book has happened over a year or two. And what an interesting couple of years it has been in respect to the anti-police sentiment. As a matter of fact, I thought I was done with this section and I find myself again having to change it because of another officer involved shooting and uprising. We as a country continue to experience tremendous amounts of protests and even riots revolving around cases such as the shooting of Michael Brown by Officer Darren Wilson, the death of Eric Garner in New York after a struggle during arrest over untaxed cigarette sales, the in-custody death of Freddie Grey, and the ridiculous blanket arrests of the officers who came into contact with him. People have begun to suddenly rebel and resist, both verbally and physically, thinking they can resist just because they decide it's not a valid arrest. Then at the end of this writing there was a shooting in Louisiana of a black male, and a week or two later near me in St. Anthony. In both cases, there was video of and/or after the shooting, which included seeing the individuals actually die. I don't think the public was ready to watch that. The videos set off an unprecedented reaction, which led to the assassination of several officers in Dallas and around the country. And each time I go back to update a few portions of this story, I continue to read about killings and ambushes of officers, protests, and even riots about officer-involved shootings that were justified. We are at an extreme division in this country between the police and the community, and the media seems to amplify the division. So, I think now is the time to share my story.

On the other end of the scale, there is a tremendous public support for police too, but not at the same outspokenness level as the anti-police groups. If someone finds out I was a police officer, I am generally thanked. My department, the Anoka County Sheriff's Office, often gets things dropped off in appreciation from the community. Recently I was the MC for the second year in a row for the local Law Enforcement Appreciation Event. And for the second year in a row we had well over one thousand people in attendance and we raised almost $15,000 for various law enforcement support charities. It was truly heartwarming to be there and it reminded me why I need to keep this book moving forward.

CHAPTER 20
ACKNOWLEDGING PTSD

I was aware of PTSD prior to this, but considered it
something that impacted only military people involved in acts
of war. It didn't occur to me that I may have had PTSD in my
situation early on. I recognize it now obviously and know I
will have to face my PTSD head on and that's exactly what I
have been doing. More importantly, I have to accept it. That
was tough for me at first. I felt there are all these soldiers
and other Police Officers who have far more dynamic
situations that are more appropriate reasons for having
"PTSD." Early on I felt like I was being disrespectful to them
by repeating that I suffer from PTSD. And I think by finally
accepting, I can accept it will be manageable, which it now
is. I can calm down easier and faster these days. I can better
control and manage my lock jaw through breathing, thought
control, and massage techniques. Repetitive sounds still do
drive me nuts sometimes, the same as the sound of
silverware screeching as they rub on a plate sends fire down
my spine, but part of managing my PTSD it is recognizing
the triggers and my limitations, and taking a different path as
needed. And for friends and family close to me, I'm very
open and honest about my triggers so they can help me
avoid them or at least help me manage them when I'm
exposed to them. Mowing the lawn still is part of my calming

process, and a massage every couple of weeks helps a lot. And once or twice a year, I'll still enjoy a good cigar with a close friend. And when I need to be, I'm open about my PTSD to people. I refuse to feel shame anymore.

As for the shooting itself, if you can't yet tell, I'm at peace with it. I no longer obsess about the idea that someone almost took my life. I lived and it's important I don't let that second chance at life go to waste because of anger. I don't hold any kind of ill will against Erik Nylen for his part in the shooting that morning. A lot of people are surprised when I say that. Honestly, he's paid the biggest price he could possibly pay, which was his life. And the truth is, it was obvious to me that he practiced for that moment all his life. So, as cliché as it sounds, it was two warriors in an unfortunate battle probably decided by fraction of a second. I truly believe Erik Nylen would understand that. And because of that, the idea of taking a life doesn't bother me so much, especially since it was a "him or me" scenario. My Sheriff didn't like that analogy, but he also had not been through that kind incident and didn't understand the true components of battle, especially close quarters combat. Nor was he there staring down the barrel of that 45 caliber. So, honestly, with all the respect in my heart, Rest In Peace Erik Nylen. I often think of his family and wonder how they are doing. I too have lost a lot of people way too early in life for a variety of reasons, so I can only imagine how this all came to them and so unexpectedly. I remember Sergeant Longbehn grumbling at his desk one day the year after the shooting and then told me to come into his office. He was reading the Anoka County Union, our local newspaper, dated May 14,

2004. Yes, my birthday, and a day after the shooting anniversary, although this was all happening a few days later. He showed me the paper and pointed out something in there. It was a memorial from Erik Nylen's family. It featured a picture of him and said this:

> *"In memory of Erik D. Nylen 11-22-73 - 5-13-03. Shot and killed in his own home by an Anoka County Sheriff's Deputy Officer one year ago at the age of 29 years. Son, we love, and miss you. Your life was full and rich in so many ways. You touched and affected the lives of so many people in your short time here on earth.*
>
> *You were called to Our Lord very unexpectedly, now your soul rests in his glory, forever. Love and our prayers from all your family, and friends."* [6]

I see what Sergeant Longbehn was bothered by as it appeared like they were attacking me and attacking my department. But I didn't take it that way. He seemed surprised when I said, "That's okay, I can respect they wrote and had that memorial published." I went on to explain that I had experienced a lot of young loss in my life and I know these memorials are published more for the healing of the family. And quite frankly, they deserve to heal. Sergeant Longbehn and I were friends so he didn't question it much further and even gave the paper to me for my own files. And

---

[6] Anoka County Union, "In Memory of Erik D. Nylen," *Anoka County Union Ad space* ,May 14, 2004.

I even think about it that way today. And I hope, almost fifteen years later, Erik Nylen's family has had the opportunity to find some kind of healing. They deserve it.

Today I can finally talk about the shooting without alcohol in my system. I can drive by the location of the shooting without my heart feeling like it's collapsing. I can go to the shooting range and shoot a gun and be around gunshots without it affecting me. I can spend hours online debating unreasonable "internet trolls," as well as the curious or the uninformed, on social media about proper police procedure without getting worked up by their often ridiculous and emotional comments, especially when it comes to police shootings. And I enjoy the reasonable dialogue of the others on there. Since active police officers deal enough with that during their shifts and often don't want to expose themselves online as a police officer, I feel that I can serve them and give back by doing what I can to educate people to the bigger picture.

Probably the last remaining remnants of stress and anger in me have revolved around the Sheriff, the Undersheriff, and the Human Resources Manager. For the longest time I thought I would never be able to finally let those go. But I figured that, for my own emotional health, I needed to find a way to get past the feeling of betrayal. I held on the desire and "need" for an apology, which goes a long way in my world. In 2010, when I heard the Sheriff was retiring, I even sent him a letter directly asking for his help in my healing by delivering a much deserved apology, preferably while he was still in office. He didn't send it or even respond to it. Anyone who knew about it asked if I thought he would actually give me an apology. And my answer is always yes. First, all of the legal and settlement dynamics were done and completed, so there was no risk to him or the county to do so. And second, as a Captain in my Patrol Division he was an amazing Captain, both fair and firm. He was a good man who wasn't clouded by politics. So I truly thought I could appeal to that man inside of him. But apparently I was wrong and I never received that apology or acknowledgement. And I guess it's possible he never received it. But I doubt that. And quite frankly, without being asked to, current Anoka County Sheriff James Stuart did a good job of opening the door to healing by simply acknowledging the mistakes made as a department. So, although I did not receive an apology from the now retired Sheriff Andersohn, or an apology from him as a citizen, the official acknowledgement by current Sheriff Stuart was a huge show of care and respect.

There are three people I knew I could go the rest of my life without interacting with, and I don't see the three of them much at all. I've seen our Human Resources Manager at a couple of open houses, but we didn't talk. I used to have to get my updated retired ID from her, but that's all pretty much an automated system now, which skips that interaction. I may not like her, but I'll give her this, she's definitely good at her job in representing the Agency and knows how to build her value with an Agency. As for the Sheriff, we've had a few bump into each other moments. We spoke at a little memorial event for Deputy Tony Fitzloff, one of my training officers when I started. Amazingly I brought up some serious concerns and mentioned that I was speaking to him as the man he was when he was my Captain, not my Sheriff. I'll give him credit, we had a mutually respectful talk, and neither of us got upset. And amazingly, he seemed to take that knowledge of the concerns and changed some of his decisions to help calm the situation with the Deputies. Honestly, that was unexpected. Then I saw him at a wedding I was working at. He tried to come and joke with me, but I avoided him. At the time I was still in a lot of pain and was having none of that. Recently I saw him again, just before the thirteenth anniversary of my shooting. It was at the Retired Officer Training where retired officers qualify to carry their firearms if they choose to. It is held each year in both May and September. I usually go to the May training and I had never seen him or the now retired Undersheriff, so I assumed they went in September. I didn't even realize he was there this year until the end when I noticed that one guy with long hair and a goatee, far from the look I always knew him to have. He appeared to dress the way drug task force guys would, so I thought I might know him. Then I realized who it was and decided to avoid him completely. And he apparently did the same.

Undersheriff King was also at this shoot. He tried to say hi to me right before it started and I pretended not to hear him. Then I thought a lot about it as I was waiting for my turn to shoot. I had been doing a lot of speaking events lately and talked often about knowing I needed to move on. I've been focused on trying to share with people about change and how positive change is within ourselves. Yet, here I was holding myself in that same mental prison by my own actions of holding a grudge. At the end of that shoot training, he re-approached me and held out his hand to shake it. I shook his hand without hesitation this time and he asked how things were and that it was good to see me. We chatted briefly and it was kind of like it used to be, except for my distrust of him of course. But it was a good start. I do realize he was put in a no-win situation when we were going through all of that.

CHAPTER 21
LIFE BEYOND THE BADGE

It's amazing that, after recalling my experience, I was able to find a healthy life beyond the badge. But thankfully it happened. My marriage survived and healed through some counseling and self-reflection on both our parts. And my family today is strong. My oldest son just finished his first year of college and I chose to return to finish my four-year degree, which I'd been close to finishing when I walked away from it after the shooting. My two younger boys are doing well too. Each of them, at their own pace and in their own way, periodically ask about the shooting and about the "bad guy." I'm fairly honest with them. I acknowledge that he is dead, but I don't spend time bashing Erik Nylen. Instead, I communicate that he died from his injuries and there is no point in holding a grudge or being angry. I tell them that I'm not happy about the shooting, nor am I sad, but, as a Police Officer, sometimes you are faced with very difficult decisions that you often have to make in a split second. I explain that I try to live my life to the fullest and enjoy every minute I can. Amazingly they seem to understand, which furthers the healing process for me.

One day I did my weekly stop at the Animal Humane Society to get my periodic dog fix because I'm a dog lover and missed owning one. On this day they had some puppies in there and that's when little Ruby entered my life. This Golden Retriever/Golden Lab mix has been a blessing and so smart and loveable. Thankfully, she does not bark or whine unnecessarily, which are common triggers of my PTSD. Sometimes it's almost like she knows my struggle and wants to help. That being said, I have to pay attention when she's intently staring at me or panting a little more than usual, because that often means she has to go outside. Sometimes I call her my unofficial therapy dog. And for that unconditional love, she receives lots of love in return.

I now own a Professional DJ and Photo Booth Company that is successful. I'm a Certified Hypnotist and focus mostly on comedy stage performances. I have the honor of bringing laughter to thousands of people each year. My job now is far different than being a Deputy Sheriff and I don't get to help people in the way I used to. But there is something enjoyable and therapeutic about making people laugh. The entertainment business allows me to use my confident and sometimes quirky sense of humor in a different way than I did in law enforcement. And I also started providing hypnotherapy options to help others with their own struggles, from weight loss to smoking to stress and more. I used those same hypnosis principles to help myself learn to calm down, relax, and reprogram my own patterns of thought.

I've been doing quite a lot of speaking engagements, which usually include talking about my experience and PTSD. This has become a huge part of my passion. I usually customize the theme and I love being able to bring a positive message to groups of all sizes. It's fun combining the speaking with comedy and some hypnosis, focusing on how to overcome adversity with a positive mind. Just as when I was a Deputy Sheriff, I enjoy doing what I can to serve and help people. It's my new calling. Recently, after I did a speaking for the Drug Awareness and Resistance Education (D.A.R.E.) Officers Association, one of the attendees approached me and said, "Thank you so much for sharing your story." It wasn't just the words he said. Instead, it was the way he shook my hand and the affirming way he looked into my eyes. They weren't only filled with pity or empathy, but instead a true look of appreciation. He'll never know how much I appreciated that.

Everything I do in my business these days gives me a positive way of thinking. I know we've all heard the old question, "Is the glass half empty, or half full?" That truly is a great way to look at life. Every negative can be turned into something positive. Or at least the positives in any situation can be focused on helping to manage through the negative. They may not be as big of positives as we often hope them to be, but there is often a positive in most situations. And, just as I learned, I share that we can't focus on changing other people, and we can only control how we react to the situation and change ourselves. So that's my focus now and it feels like a powerful way of thinking.

But there was one thing missing; one final step to healing that I began to realize during my speaking events and writing. The more speaking events I did, and the more I worked on writing this book, the more I became aware of this final need. I'd been holding a well-deserved grudge. But I have started to realize something I would label as "interesting." My anger and my grudge weren't affecting any of them. My anger and grudge did not impact their lives, not even one little bit. That was a huge wake-up call. In spring 2016 I realized that to truly find my final healing, I must find a way to forgive. I forgave Mr. Nylen because he had already paid the price. But my anger over my administration was such a powerful negative energy that had led to the last thirteen years of my life being consumed. Once I realized I needed to forgive I just needed to find the ability. And I knew that would be when I finished writing this book. So I mulled it over it for a couple of months literally talking to myself about it. And simply in talking about the idea felt good. So on the thirteenth anniversary of the shooting I was ready. And I found my platform on social media. Here's what I wrote.

> "Today marks thirteen years. Not an unlucky number to me. Thirteen years ago I was lying in a hospital bed sharing laughter, tears, and everything in between with many of you. And an interesting thirteen years it has been with many PTSD roller coasters. I appreciate you guys riding that train with me.
>
> I can honestly say that this has been the most peaceful anniversary to date; one that I didn't spend the entire night and tonight intoxicated to make sure it was all a blur. Instead, it has been one of peace. I spent the day in two of the most peaceful places I've ever been in my life. And now I am flying home to be with friends and family this weekend. Is not only the shooting anniversary, but tomorrow I turn forty-four.
>
> I want everyone to know that the steps I've taken over the last couple of years are paying off. Talking about

it, getting healthy (working on my weight), writing about it, organizing my mind, and ultimately freeing my emotions has been amazing. I have one step left.

I've learned in my many speaking engagements and discussions that we can't control others or make others do what we want. All I wanted was an apology. But we can only control our part of anything we are involved in. So it's time for me to fully and finally take control of what I can personally control.

I recognize, in my mind, that the three people I'm mad at don't necessarily deserve my forgiveness. But being mad and holding a grudge doesn't affect them whatsoever. It only affects me...and affects me negatively. It damages me...and the anger injures me. It holds me in a prison cell that I deserve to be free of. I recognize I'm now the only one who holds me in that prison cell. Nobody else. So here goes...

Just as I forgave Eric Nylen for his actions the night if my shooting...

To those who I felt anger towards in the midst of all this...I forgive you."

The release when I posted that was so amazingly healing. The rest of the day I felt enlightened. I felt calm. I felt at peace.

CHAPTER 22
FINAL THOUGHTS

I have spent quite a bit of time trying to figure out the best way to wrap up my story in this book. I'll settle with my final thoughts. Knowing what I've been through people often want to know if I miss being a police officer. The answer is a big fat YES! I feel like I was made for that job. I was good at it. That much I am sure about. People ask how I feel about the Anoka County Sheriff's Office. The answer is I love my department and it is filled with many great police officers. Administrations will come and go, but the department will always be a special part of me. And the current Sheriff, James Stuart, and his administration have been good for the department and for the community. It is good to see that it doesn't have to be one side or the other. That there can be a common ground and a balance between leading a department and representing a community. I think a lot of police leadership could really learn a lot from Sheriff Stuart.

In my seven years with Anoka County, and ten years as a whole in the Law Enforcement field, I got to do a lot. I negotiated my way into a significant amount of training and I have such a vast set of experiences because of that and the type and size of my department at the time. And as I said earlier, because of the things I focused on, I really believe I made a difference in my community, even if only a small one. I've never been big on the idea of fate, but I was there for a purpose. Maybe I was supposed to be there at that moment, at that time. Maybe my path of life took me to that moment, so one of the other two Deputies that called in that night didn't lose their life. Or maybe my path took me there so that a Deputy who was two days on her own didn't have to face that violent encounter alone and possibly lose her life. Or maybe it was simply just a series of unfortunate events that came together by chance. We will never know.

Sam describes it best when she says, "I feel like that night you saved my life and I saved yours." That may sound strange to many people, but not to me. That conversation happened after years of processing for each of us. Sam definitely helped save my life that night and I was a part of saving hers, which is an interesting thought. It's not something I want to gloat about, but I'm glad I was there because I couldn't bear the possible alternative. And in many ways her friendship through the years after has saved me. Maybe not my life, but my emotions. Recently I met her twin daughters at a Law Enforcement Appreciation Event I was the Master of Ceremonies for. They were born after the shooting and were not aware of the incident their mom and I had been in so I was careful about what I said and the emotions I was showing. But as I shook their hands and hugged them, it took everything in me to hold back my tears. It was such a special moment for me and they are both beautiful young ladies. Sam wasn't there at that moment so I sent her a picture of us at the event. She sent a warm and excited response because I finally got to meet her nuggets.

Sam has left the Anoka County Sheriff's Office. Based on stories she told me that I wasn't previously aware of, I can only say I understand. After her girls were born she decided to re-enter the field of law enforcement and was hired by the Fillmore County Sheriff's Officer in Southern Minnesota. She was hired as a jailer and dispatcher and says she originally had no desire to return to street patrol or that part of law enforcement. But her Sheriff at the time eventually convinced her to take it further. She is now the first full-time female deputy for that department. She's also a union steward and a negotiator. She recently graduated with her Masters in Criminal Justice and just prior to the release of this book Sam started teaching. She is now a Professor of Criminal Justice at Winona State University in Southeast Minnesota. To say I'm proud is an understatement. And I find it even more enjoyable that we both seem to be on a positive path of healing and success. We both deserve that.

I mentioned earlier that I was made to understand that the Sheriff was upset by the fact that I took a life and that I didn't seem bothered by it. Maybe I didn't show it outwardly enough, but I didn't take the death of Mr. Nylen lightly at all. I was merely going through a process of managing my emotions regarding his death and nearly dying myself. And honestly, the Sheriff and his administration's actions made it nearly impossible to process everything effectively. I've been involved in saving lives before, multiple times. It's a part of the job. I've seen many dead bodies and many suicides, which again is a part of the job. I've also attempted to save lives where I wasn't successful. I've had someone attempt to take my life before, this the closest to actually happening.

And now, as we've discussed, I've taken a life. These are all things that will be a part of me for the rest of my time here on earth. Eric Nylen will be a part of me for the rest of my life.

My understanding of life and death is not one I wish upon anyone. But I also recognize that life must move forward, regardless of the obstacles placed in front of us. And life must move forward, because if we don't, IF I DON'T, all of those experiences…my near death…the life I took in order to live…would all be for northing.

"Blessed are the peace makers, for they shall be called the Children of God"
Matthew 5:9

To schedule Dustin for a speaking event
or inquire about other projects and events

Reichert Productions, Inc.
Dustin A. Reichert
www.DustinReichert.com • info@DustinReichert.com

Dustin & Sam (2016)

Dustin and Sheriff James Stuart at the 2nd Annual
Law Enforcement Appreciation Event (2016)

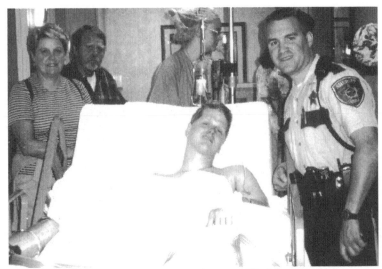

Dustin on the way to surgery along with his mom, his uncle and partner/friend, Deputy Hlavinka (2003)

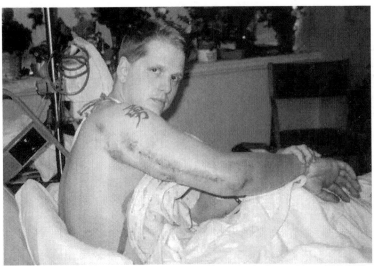

Dustin in hospital two days after the shooting (2003)

Dustin taking his Oath of Office and being Sworn-In by
Sheriff Larry Podany (1998)

Dustin & oldest son (2000)

Dustin receiving Purple Heart from Undersheriff King and Sheriff Andersohn (2004)

Dustin with Sgt. Scott Nolan, Anoka PD (left) and Sgt. Jon Urquhart, Coon Rapids PD (right) at the awards ceremony (2004)

Dustin and his family

Dustin and Ruby

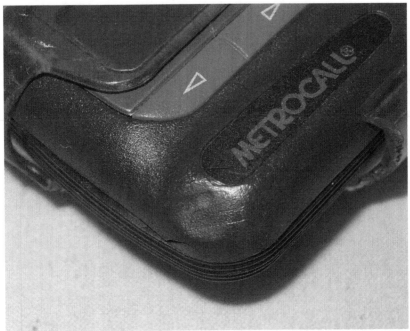

Pager that deflected the bullet and changed its path

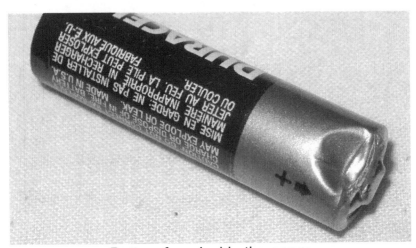

Battery from inside the pager

SPECIAL THANKS TO:

Deputy Ed Whitledge
pictured here with his K9 Partner Bud
Ramsey County Sheriff's Office
(Retired)

Made in the USA
Middletown, DE
22 January 2017